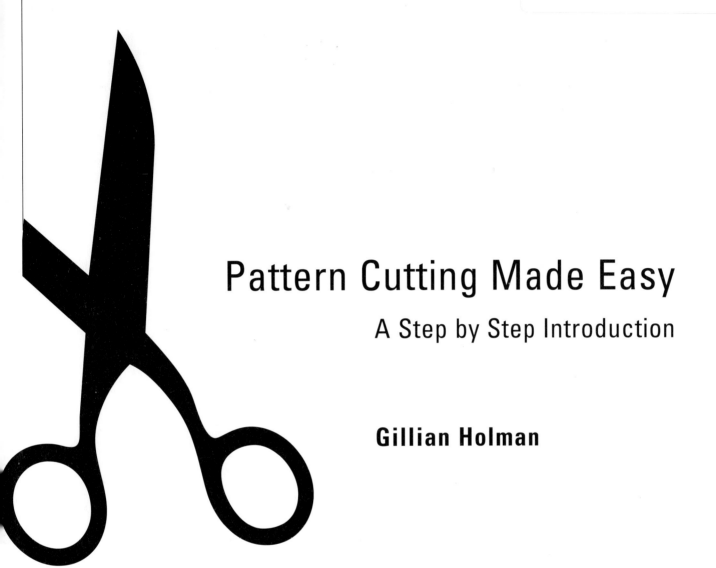

Pattern Cutting Made Easy

A Step by Step Introduction

Gillian Holman

B T Batsford Ltd, London

© Gillian Holman 1997
First published 1997
Reprinted 2000

Printed by Butler and Tanner, Frome.

for the publisher

B.T Batsford Ltd
9 Blenheim Court
Brewery Road
London N7 9NT

A member of the Chrysalis Group plc

A CIP catalogue record for this book is available from the British Library.

ISBN 0 7134 8093 9

Contents

Introduction   5

Skirt Pattern Cutting   6

Basic Skirt Block   8

Four-Gore Skirt   10

Skirt with Yoke   12

Skirt with Flounce   14

Six-Gore Skirt   16

Skirt with Inverted Pleats   18

Skirt with Box Pleats   20

Skirt with Knife Pleat   22

Skirt with Inset Pleat   24

Peg Top Skirt   26

Circular Skirt   28

Culottes   30

Hip/Yoke Pocket   32

In-Seam Pocket   34

Bodice Pattern Cutting   36

Fitted Bodice Block   38

Bodice Draft   40

Loose Fitting Bodice Block   42

Buttonstands and Facings   44

Bodice with Yoke   46

Basque Waist Bodice   48

Pleated Front Bodice   50

Princess Line Bodice   52

Crossover Bodice   54

Bodice with Aysmmetric Opening   56

Double Breasted Opening   58

Deep Cowl Neck Line   60

High Cut Cowl   62

Fly Front Opening   64

Necklines and Facings   66

Collars   68

Sleeve Pattern Cutting   78

Sleeve Block   80

Semi-Fitted Sleeve Block   81

Tightly Fitted Sleeve   82

Bishop Sleeve with Deep Cuff   84

Leg O'Mutton Sleeve   86

Raised Crown   88

Two-Piece Sleeve   90

Plain Short Sleeve   92

Puffed Sleeve   92

Bell Sleeve   94

Sleeve Gathered at the Head   94

Sports Sleeve   96

Saddle Sleeve   98

Kimono Sleeve   100

Deep Raglan Sleeve   102
Cap Sleeve   104

Jacket Block   106

Tailored Collar   108

Trouser Block   110

Supplies and Suppliers   112

Introduction

This book is designed for use by part-time students of fashion who do not have constant access to their tutors or for competent home dressmakers. It is not intended for advanced students but for those who need a firm grounding in the principles of pattern drafting.

Direct measurement block pattern instructions are included at the beginning of each section, but it must be stressed that for the home dressmaker a commercial shell pattern is much easier to use. Direct methods should only be attempted with a tutor available to advise.

While teaching part-timers over a number of years, I have found that the several excellent pattern cutting books produced are too complicated to follow without a tutor constantly available to explain. The diagrams and texts included here have been produced as a result of my part-time students' struggles and only finalized when they have found it possible to understand when working alone.

Buy the shell nearest to your own measurements and cut it out following the instructions provided. It is well worth the time to get a friend to measure your body accurately and to adjust the paper pattern before putting it on fabric. Having done so, cut out in calico and make up. Correct any fitting faults and mark clearly. When you are happy with the fit, take it apart and cut away all seams and darts.

Now place your calico pieces on to card and draw round them accurately. Be sure to put in all markings, straight grain and notches (balance marks).

Darts, particularly the bust darts, must now be adjusted from dressmaker's darts to pattern cutter's darts, that means that they must be extended. All bust darts should meet at the bust point. Hip and bodice darts extend by 2.5 cm (1") at their point. Once your patterns have been cut, return to the dressmaker's dart, throwing the fullest area of fabric into the fullest area of the body. All patterns are made without seam allowances from your block. If you prefer to work with seam allowances, they are added only when the pattern is finalized but before cutting the fabric.

Students are advised to invest in a good dressmaking manual with clear diagrams and text to help them with garment construction. British Standard measurements are included in these books and are also shown in commercial pattern books and on pattern sleeves.

Skirt Pattern Cutting

All pattern cutting derives from a basic block pattern. This may be a standard size, most easily made from a commercial shell pattern, or a personal block, cut to individual measurements and fitted accurately in calico before being transferred to card. This is time consuming but well worth the effort.

A basic skirt is straight cut with one dart either side at the front and back. For a curvy shape, use two small darts either side at front and back, see sketches below.

The straight grain is centre front and centre back, **figs 1, 2**, and the side seams should be at right angles to the floor, **fig 3**. If this is not so, lift either the front or back of the garment at the waist until the garment hangs correctly and adjust the waist fit accordingly. A good dressmaking manual or a commercial shell pattern will give clear fitting instructions.

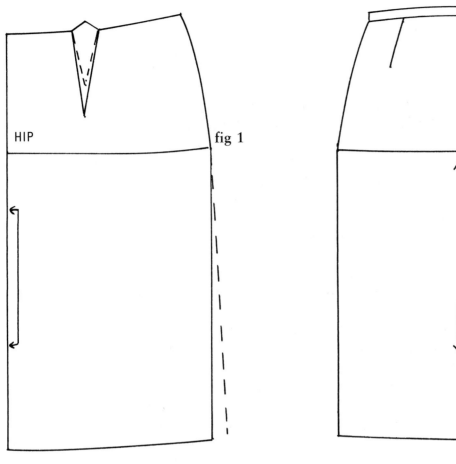

HIP   fig 1

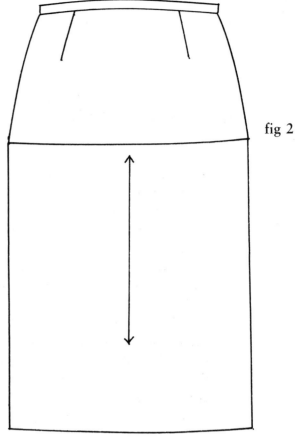

fig 2

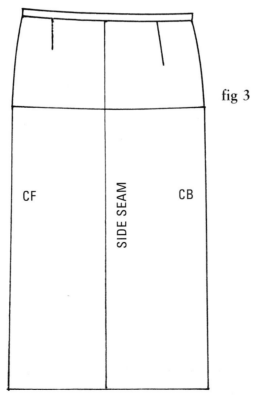

fig 3

CF   SIDE SEAM   CB

Basic Skirt Block

Take accurate measurements for the waist (at the narrowest part of the body), hip (the widest part of the body, *not* the hipbone level), hip depth (from waist to hip at the side seam), skirt length (waist to knee), and waist to floor.

Add the following to the body measurements for ease before dividing for a quarter pattern: 5-6 cm (2-2⅜") at hip, 2.5 cm (1") at waist.

Skirt Back

A-B Skirt length from waist to knee.

A-C Hip depth.

C-D Quarter of hip measurement including ease. For hip of 93 cm (36⅝"), add 5 cm (2") ease. Quarter of 98 cm (38⅝") = 24.5 cm (9⅝").

B-E Equals C-D.

E-F Equals A-B.

A-G Quarter of waist measurement including ease + 3 cm (1⅛") dart (4 cm [1⅝"] for size 16 and above, or for a very small waist).

G-H 1.25 cm (½") up from line A-F.

A-H Waist line curve. Lower at C-B by 1 cm (⅜") and curve up at the side seam.

H-D Draw a straight line from H to D. Mark out 1 cm (⅜") at centre and curve for hip.

For sizes 10/12/14 mark a dart 10/11/12 cm (4/4⅜/4¾") along the waist from point A. For larger sizes, move the dart out towards the hip by 6 mm (¼") per size. Draw a vertical line to the level of the hipbone, approximately 12-13 cm (4¾-5⅛"), and mark 1.5 cm (⅝") either side of this for a dart for smaller sizes. If the dart is too large to fit smoothly, divide to make two smaller darts. For larger sizes, draw a dart of 2 cm (¾") either side of this line. At point E, the side seam/hem, mark up 5 mm (¼") and curve the hem.

Skirt Front

Trace off the skirt back and shorten the darts from their point by approximately 2 cm (¾").

Raise at the centre front by 5 mm (¼") and take off to nothing at the side seam (see dotted line). Adjust to new waistline.

If the wearer has a large stomach, take 5 mm (¼") from the front side seam and extend back by 5 mm (¼"). Reverse the procedure for a large bottom.

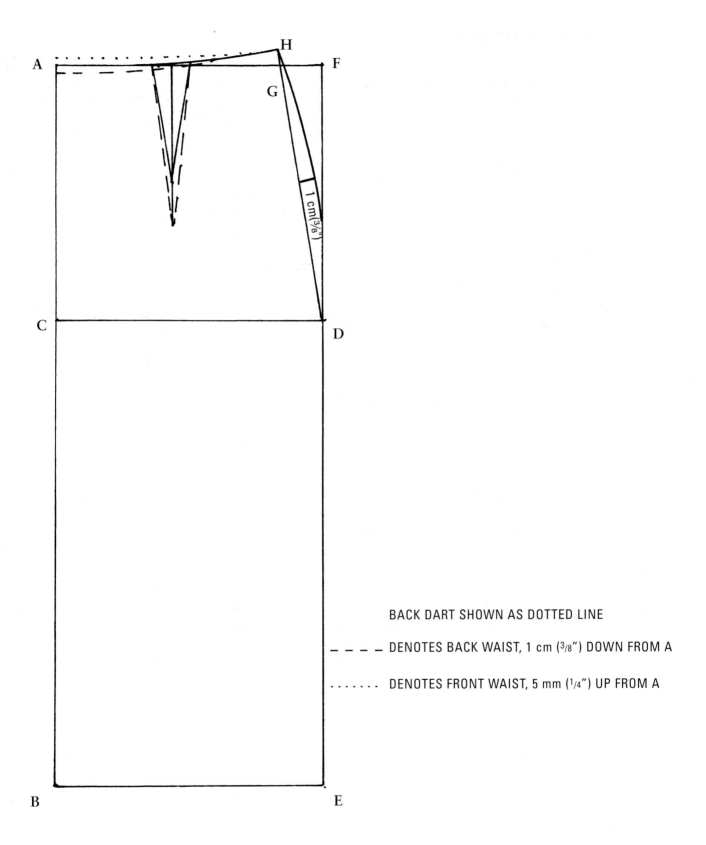

1 cm(3/8")

BACK DART SHOWN AS DOTTED LINE

– – – – DENOTES BACK WAIST, 1 cm (3/8") DOWN FROM A

. . . . DENOTES FRONT WAIST, 5 mm (1/4") UP FROM A

Four-Gore Skirt

1 Outline the skirt block, mark in hipline and add balance marks (notches) at this point.

2 Divide in half at hip and hem, mark a line through these points and extend to the waist. Move the dart onto this line, **fig 1**.

3 Slash up this line and fold out the dart, opening up the hem, **fig 2**. The pattern must lie flat.

4 Redraw the pattern with the grain at the centre of the panel, **fig 3**. It may be necessary to straighten the hip curve slightly (see dotted line).

5 By shifting the straight grain to the centre of the panel the fullness will hang evenly around the body and not to the sides as in an A-line garment.

6 If front and back blocks are very similar, the same pattern may be used for all pieces. If not, cut a back and a front pattern.

Waistband

This should be cut to the measurement of the waist of the garment, not to the waist of the wearer. The waistband should be the length of the garment waist, plus the buttonstand, by the depth wanted plus facing. If using a bulky fabric, cut only the outer waistband in the garment fabric and face with lining.

For a garment waist of 70.5 cm (27¾”) and buttonstand of 2.5 cm (1”), with a waistband depth of 2.5 cm (1”) and facing of 2.5 cm (1”), the waistband will measure 73 cm x 5 cm (28¾” x 2”).

Shaped Waistband

To allow for the figure shape above the waist, follow the instructions for the basque bodice (see pp48-9).

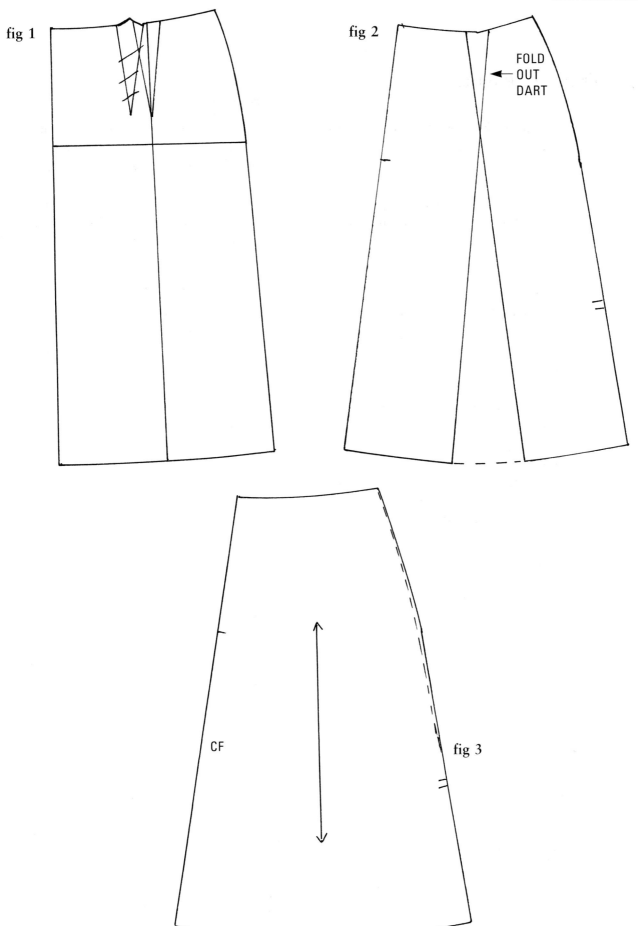

fig 1

fig 2

FOLD
OUT
DART

CF

fig 3

Skirt with Yoke

The instructions here may also be used for yokes on trousers or jeans patterns. Yokes may be cut to any shape but care should be taken to choose a style to flatter the figure of the wearer. Start with a simple shape, as shown in the diagrams opposite.

1 Outline the block, decide on the shape and position of the yoke and draw in the style line and balance marks, **fig 1**.

2 Divide in half at hip and hem, mark a vertical line through these points to the waist and move the dart onto the line, **fig 1**.

3 Slash up the line from hem to dart point. Cut away the yoke along the style line and fold out the dart, **fig 2**.

4 Adapt the lower section of skirt as for the four-gore or any other appropriate design.

5 If the dart extends into the lower section, use it as in the four-gore skirt to add fullness.

6 Redraw the yoke and skirt to soften the angles from the dart folds, **fig 3**.

The straight grain on the yoke sections should be at the centre front and centre back unless bias detail is required.

The front and back yokes need not be the same shape but they must marry at the side seams.

fig 1

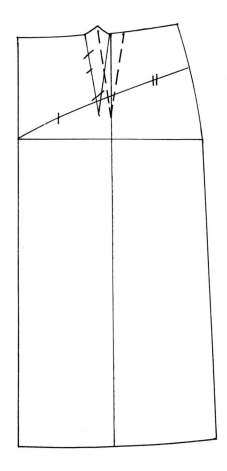

fig 2

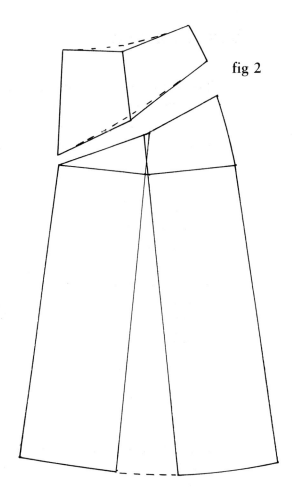

fig 3

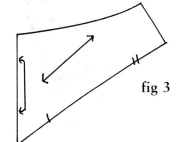

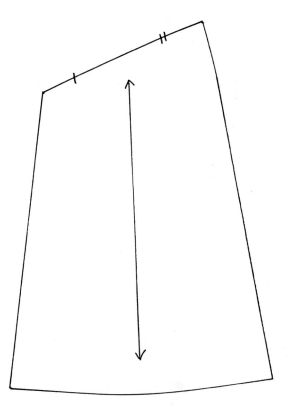

Skirt with Flounce

This style needs to be cut with the flounce in a soft fabric that drapes well. Top skirt and flounce may be cut in contrasting fabric for greater effect.

1 Outline the block and draw in style lines for the flounce to any shape or level you consider appropriate to the fabric and the wearer, **fig 1.**

2 Put in balance marks and narrow the skirt a little to make the flounce more dramatic (see the dotted line, **fig 1**).

3 Divide the flounce into equal sections, **fig 1**.

4 Cut away the flounce, slash on dividing lines and spread for fullness, **fig 2**.

5 Redraw the pattern pieces, softening the angles where the flounce has been spread, **fig 3**.

Straight grain is at the centre front and centre back of the upper garment and the centre front of the flounce or, for a softer look, the true bias is the centre front of the flounce.

It is easier to attach the curve of the flounce to the skirt if the seam line is stay-stitched and the curve clipped at intervals.

To get the full effect of this style you must spread generously for the flounce. Round to a full circle if the fabric is suitable.

fig 1

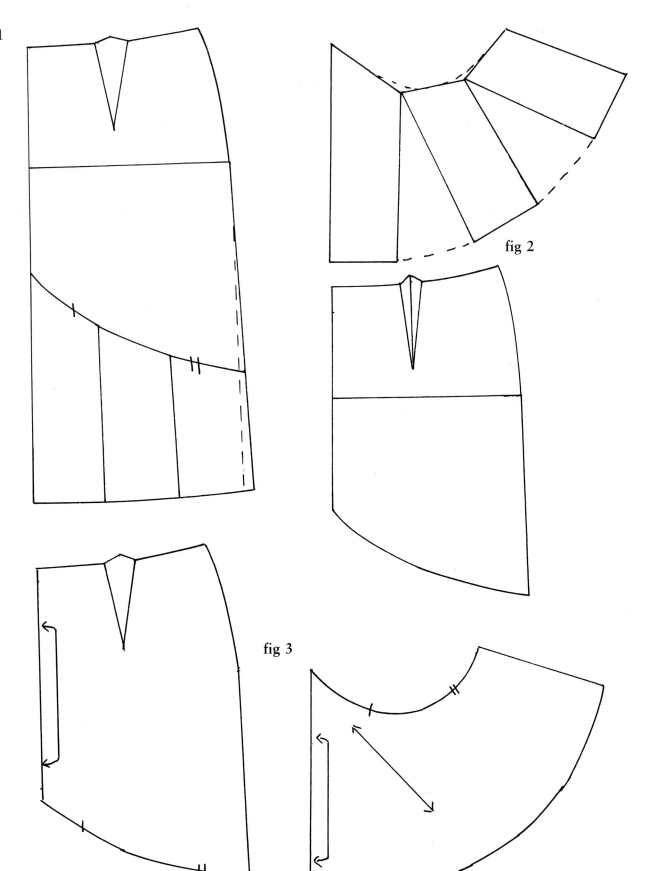

fig 2

fig 3

Six-Gore Skirt

This is an elegant style for semi-evening wear.

1 Cut full front and back blocks, not half as previously. Divide each block into three equal sections at the hip and hem and draw vertical lines through to the waist. Move the darts onto these lines, **fig 1.**

2 Mark a line where the flare will begin, **fig 1.**

3 Cut up the vertical lines and remove the dart shaping, **fig 2.** This gives a shaped seam.

4 Cut away at the flare line and divide the lower section into four equal parts. Slash and spread, **fig 3.**

5 Place this section against the lower edge of the upper skirt section, but do not overlap the pieces as this will shorten the overall length. Redraw as one pattern piece, **fig 4.**

6 Follow these instructions for each panel. When completed, you should have one centre front panel and one centre back panel, both marked 'cut 1'; and one side front and one side back panel, both marked 'cut 2'.

Straight grain is down the centre of each panel.

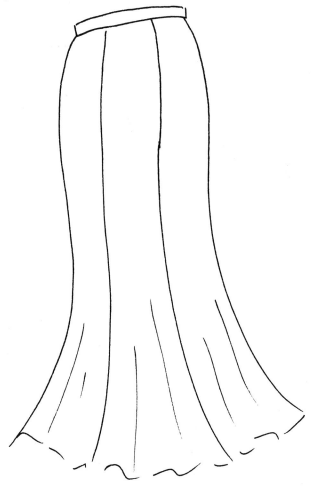

fig 1

fig 2

fig 3

fig 4

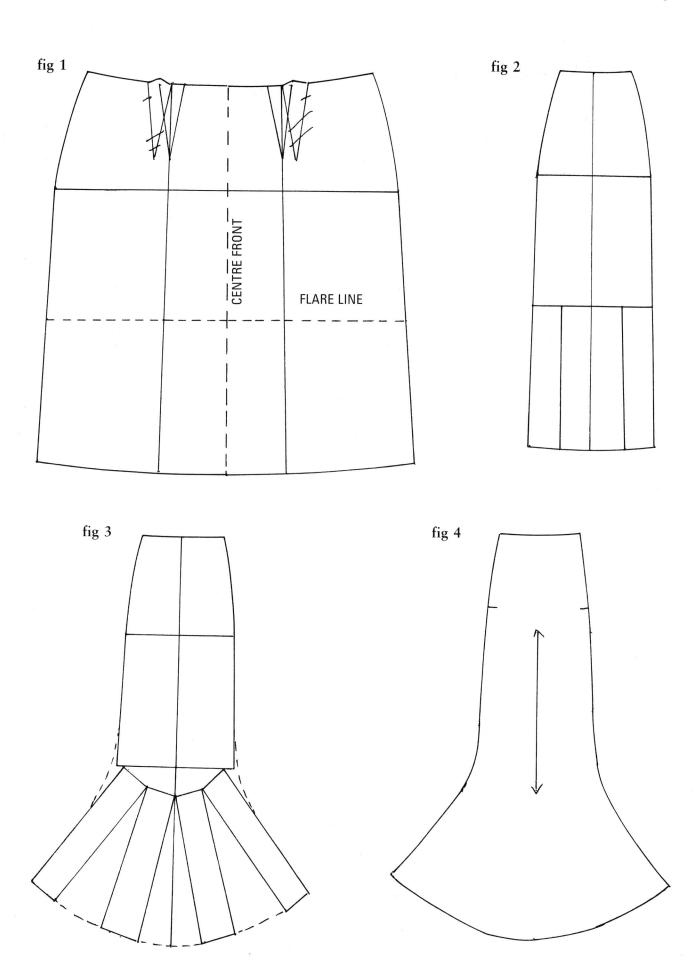

CENTRE FRONT

FLARE LINE

Skirt with Inverted Pleats

A classic tailored skirt for a suit or 'smart casual' wear, this is good in almost any reasonably firm fabric and is eternally popular in tweeds and checks.

1 Outline block. At the centre front (or centre back) add 1 cm (³/₈") at the hem and rule back to nothing at the waist, **fig 1**. This provides stride room and keeps the fold line crisp. If working in check or stripe, use an unaltered block. Straight grain remains at the centre front.

2 Decide on the width of the pleat and add double this amount to the centre front (or centre back) line. This provides both the pleat and the pleat underlay, **fig 1**.

3 Fold out pleat and underlay and cut at the waist to give the waistline curve to the top of the pleat.

4 The underlay may be cut in one with the skirt, but a crisper finish is produced by cutting it as a separate piece, **fig 2**.

Straight grain on the underlay is at the centre front line.

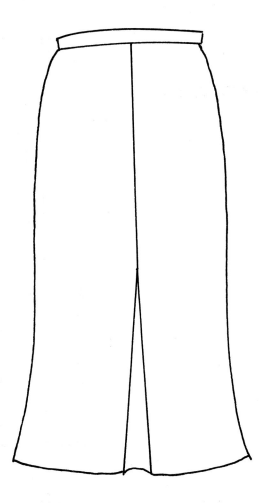

fig 1

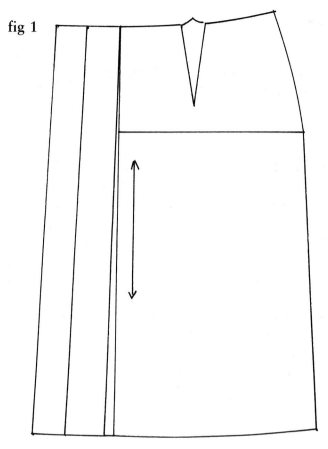

fig 2

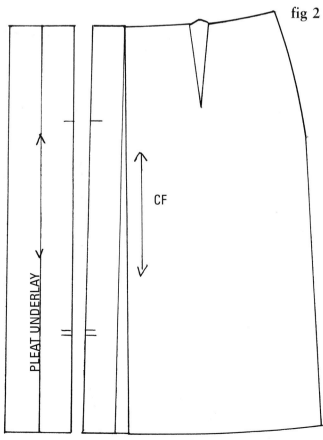

Skirt with Box Pleats

Box pleats may be used singly at the centre front or centre back, or be grouped across the skirt panel (see sketches below).

1 Follow the process for inverted pleats (pp18-19), adding stride room and pleat to the centre front or centre back line, **fig 1.**

2 Cut away the pleat section at the original centre front line, **fig 2.** This means that the seam will be hidden under the pleat.

3 If the fabric is not too bulky, darts may be moved over into the pleat line and concealed in the pleat.

Do not add stride room if using multiple pleats as this will take the grain line too far out.

fig 1

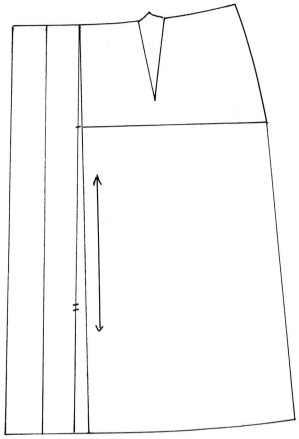

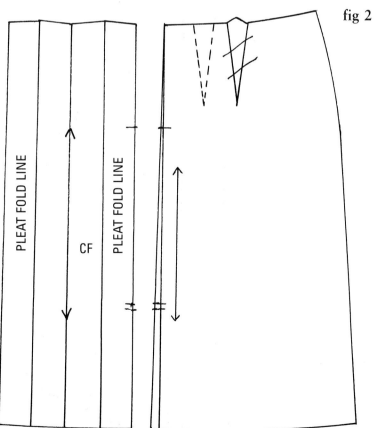

fig 2

PLEAT FOLD LINE

CF

PLEAT FOLD LINE

Skirt with Knife Pleats

This is another classic shape. The pleats can be used either centrally or asymmetrically, as in the sketch below. Checked fabrics can be pleated out for a particularly dramatic effect.

1 Outline the block. Mark in the dart lightly. Draw vertical lines where pleats are wanted, **fig 1**.

2 Slash through the pleat lines and spread the pattern equally, **fig 2**. Pleats should not overlap on the underside of a garment as this creates bulk.

3 Redraw the pattern, shading the pleated areas to avoid confusion, **fig 3**.

4 Divide the dart width between the pleats: i.e. for a 3 cm (1¹/8") dart add 1 cm (³/8") to each of three pleats to restore the shaping, **fig 3**.

5 Fold out the pleats before cutting the final pattern to ensure the shaping at the top is correct.

Join the pleated left front to the plain right front at the centre front and cut on a single thickness of fabric. The straight grain is at the centre front.

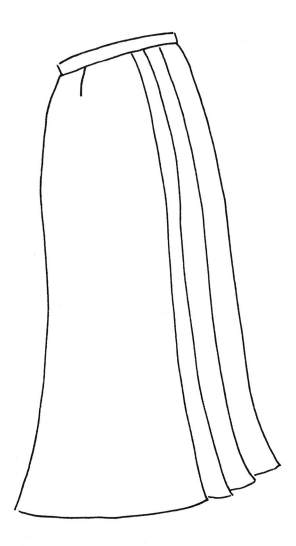

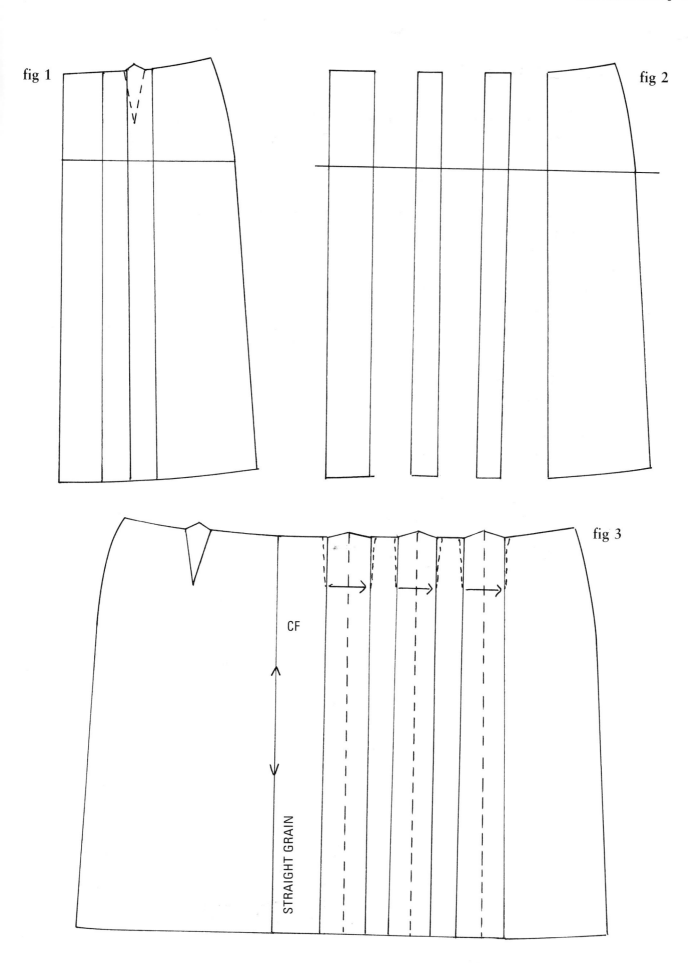

fig 1

fig 2

fig 3

CF

STRAIGHT GRAIN

Skirt with Inset Pleat

This detailing is equally attractive at the front or back of a garment. It allows stride room without spoiling the line of the skirt. If using on the skirt back, do not take the style line too high or the pleats will crush when the wearer sits down.

1 Outline the block and draw the inset style line and pleat lines. Add balance marks, **fig 1**.

2 Cut away the inset section, number the pleats and cut through the lines, **fig 2**.

3 Spread the pleat sections evenly on fresh paper to allow for the width of the pleats. Mark fold lines, **fig 2**.

4 Fold out the pleats in paper before cutting the upper edge, **fig 3**. This ensures the accuracy of the pleats at the seam, **fig 4**.

This style looks good in a medium weight wool or a linen mix. It needs a fabric with 'body' to ensure that the pleats hang well.

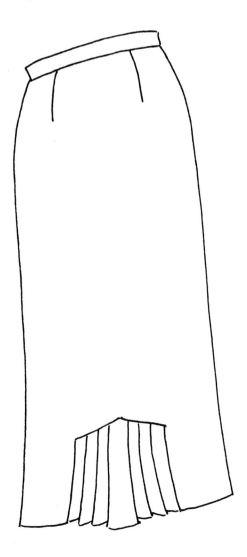

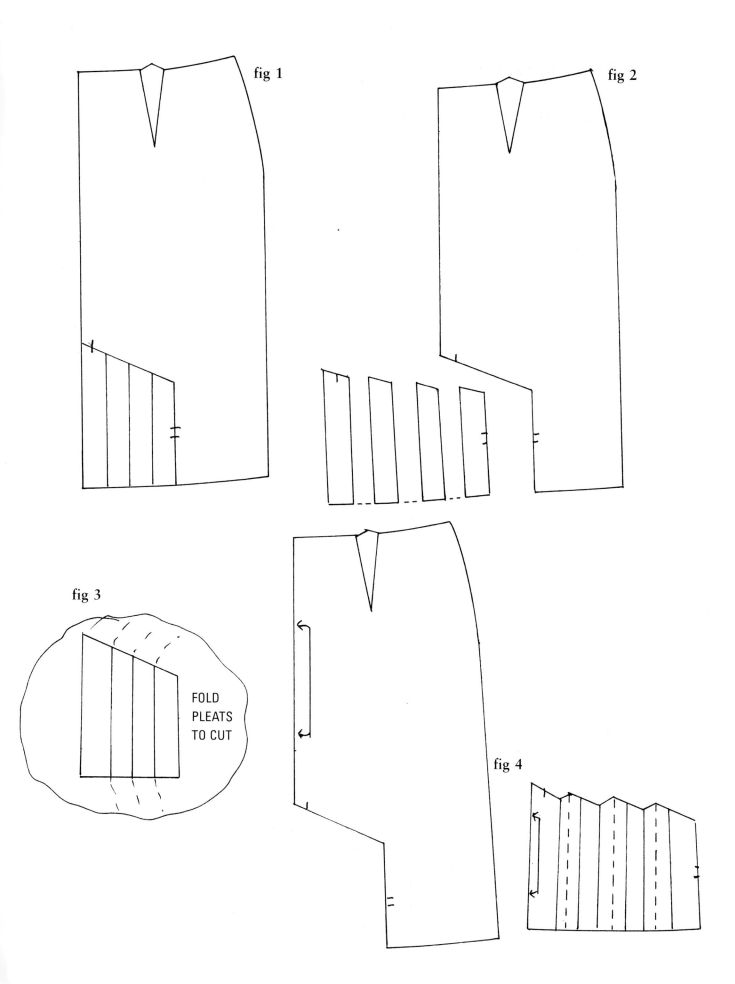

fig 1

fig 2

fig 3

FOLD
PLEATS
TO CUT

fig 4

Peg Top Skirt

This is a very fitted shape that emphasizes the waist. The peg top may be used at the front of the skirt with a plain back or with a skirt that is also pleated at the back. With the latter option, ensure that the pleats marry on the side seam and are caught to it to prevent them dropping. It may be necessary to mount the fashion fabric on a lining to give control. This style was popular with 'The New Look' of 1947 when the pleats were stiffened to draw attention to the difference between waist and hip.

1 Outline the block and narrow at the side seam from hip to hem, **fig 1**.

2 Draw curved lines from waist to hip for the pleats, **fig 1**. Do not centre the pleats over the stomach.

3 Slash and spread for the pleats, **fig 2**.

4 Redraw the pattern. Fold out the pleats before cutting the waistline to ensure accuracy at the top of the pleat, **fig 3**.

5 To incorporate the dart, move each pleat over by a third of the dart width.

Pleat fold lines should be very carefully marked on the pattern. It is worth taking the time to cut and fit in calico to correct pleats before finalizing the pattern.

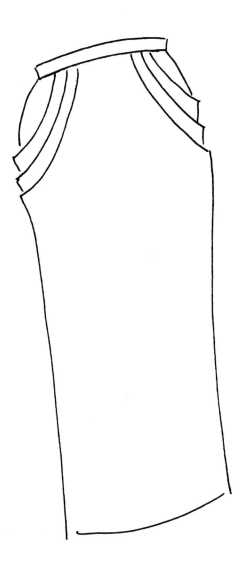

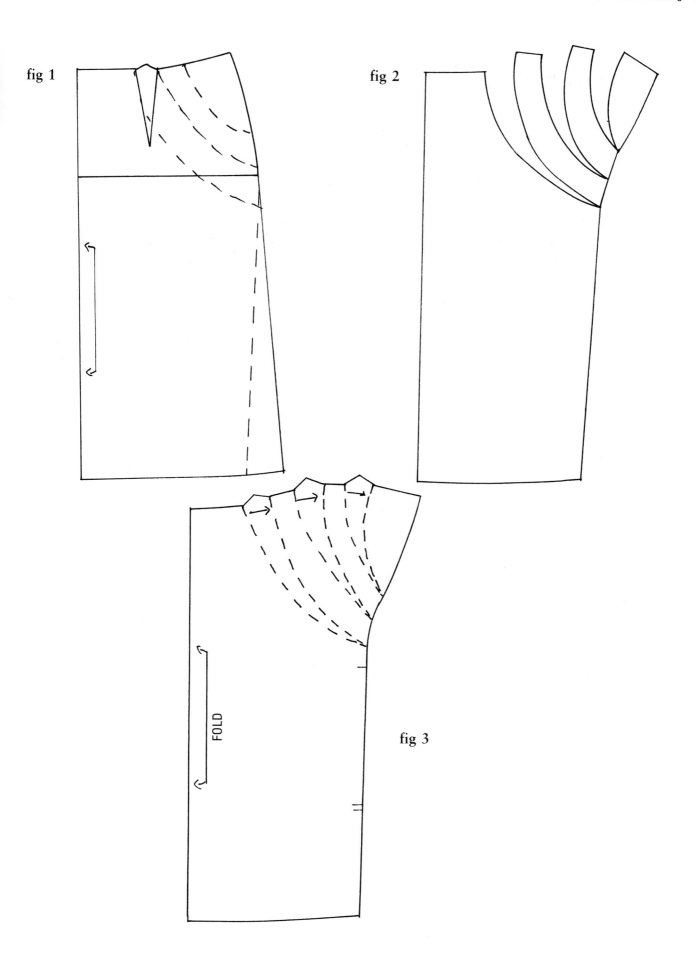

fig 1

fig 2

fig 3

FOLD

Circular Skirt

Method One

1 Take the waist measurement and add 2.5 cm (1") for ease. To find the radius for the skirt divide this measurement by 6.3. eg for a 66 cm (26") waist, add ease of 2.5 cm (1") = 68.5 cm (27"). The radius of 68.5 (27") divided by 6.3 = 10.8 cm (4¼").

2 Mark a central point for the skirt and pivot round this by the length of the radius. This is the waist of the skirt, **fig 1**.

3 Draw out the length of skirt required from the waist and mark the hem.

Method Two

1 Take a quarter of the waist measurement (including ease) and draw a rectangle the width of this measurement by the length of the skirt, **fig 2**.

2 Divide into equal sections vertically, **fig 2**.

3 Slash and spread till the outer edges are at right angles. Curve to soften the angles at the top and bottom and redraw, **fig 3**.

4 For the skirt, cut two on the fold.

Straight grain or true bias is at the centre front and centre back.

Do not forget to add seam allowance at the waist as well as at the side seams.

METHOD 1   **fig 1**   NOT TO SCALE

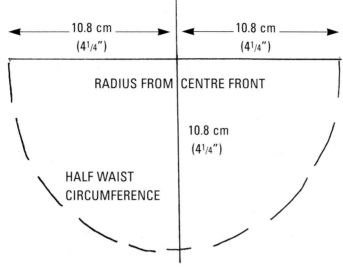

10.8 cm
(4¹/₄″)

10.8 cm
(4¹/₄″)

RADIUS FROM CENTRE FRONT

10.8 cm
(4¹/₄″)

HALF WAIST
CIRCUMFERENCE

METHOD 2   **fig 2**   **fig 3**

QUARTER WAIST

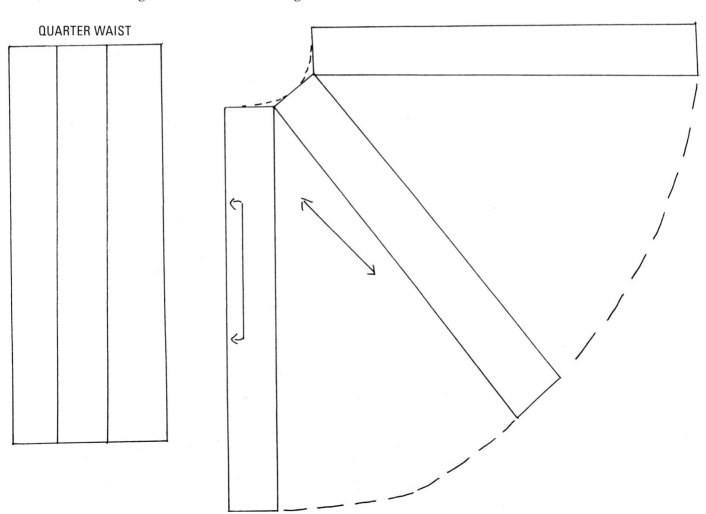

Culottes

First popular in the late 1920s, this comfortable garment has come back into fashion in the last few years and shows no signs of losing its appeal.

1 Outline front and back skirt blocks. Mark in the hip line and crotch depth, **fig 1**.

2 Front: Extend the crotch line at the centre front by a quarter of the width of the block, **fig 1**. Square down parallel with the centre front line.

3 Draw in the crotch curve 2.3 cm ($^7/_8$") from angle.

4 Back: Extend the crotch line at the centre back by a third of the block width and square down parallel to the centre back line, **fig 2**.

5 Draw in the crotch curve 2.5 cm (1") from angle.

For a pleated style, add the pleats to the centre front and/or the centre back and follow the above instructions, adding the crotch to the pleat.

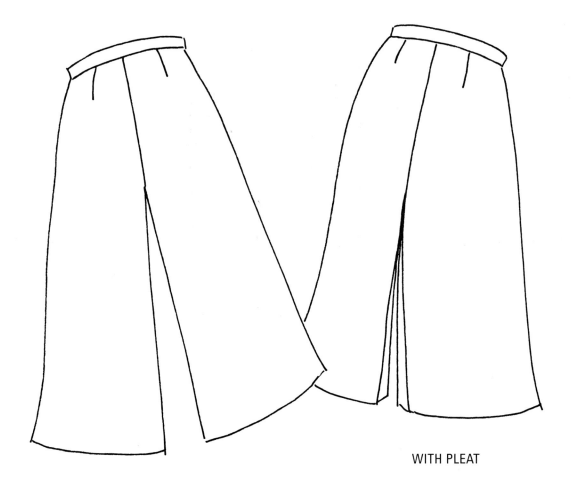

WITH PLEAT

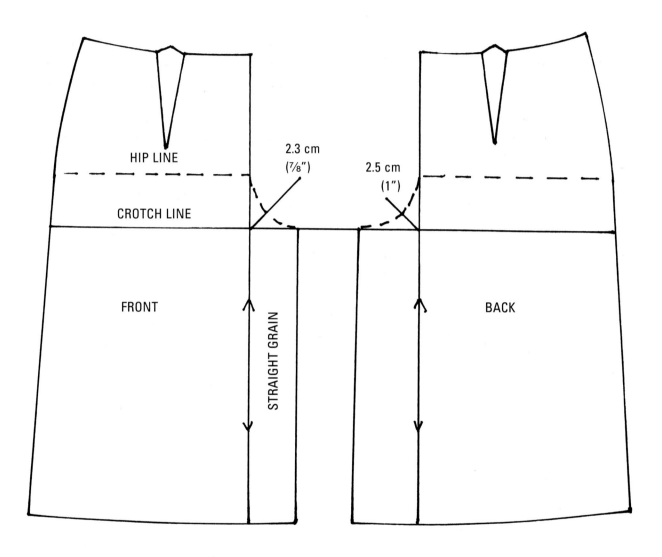

Hip/Yoke Pocket

This pocket is ideal for skirts and trousers. If using a heavy fabric it is necessary to cut the lining and/or pocket bag in a thinner fabric to prevent bulky lines on the garment.

1 Outline the block and draw in the pocket/yoke style line and the pocket bag shape, **fig 1**.

2 Trace off the pocket/yoke and the pocket bag shape and cut out, **fig 2**.

3 Cut away on the style line, **fig 2**.

4 Stitch the pocket bag to the garment, right sides together, **fig 3**. Clip and turn through. Stitch the yoke section to the bag around the lower edge, **fig 4**.

5 Tack the completed pocket/yoke in position and join up the rest of the garment.

To prevent the pocket stretching with use, stay-tape the curved seam joining the skirt and pocket bag.

If the waist darts are small it may be possible to incorporate them in the pocket shaping. Experiment in paper or calico.

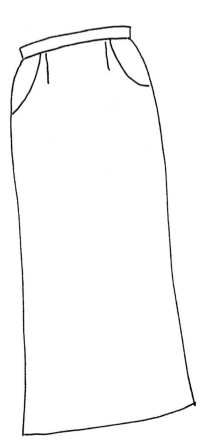
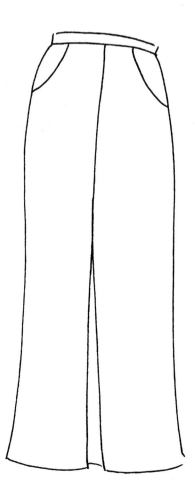

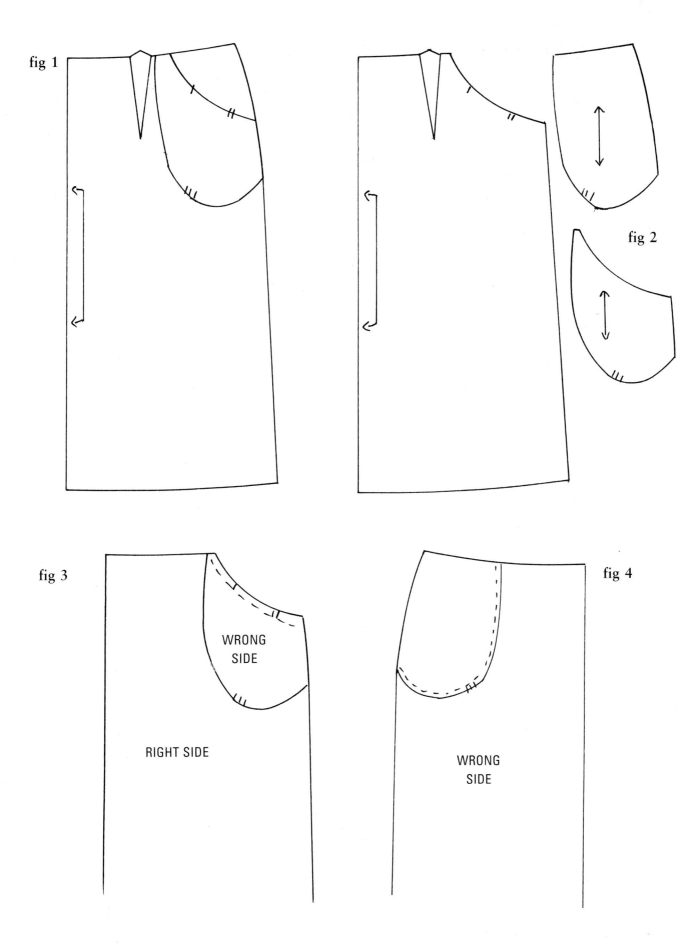

fig 1

fig 2

fig 3

WRONG
SIDE

RIGHT SIDE

fig 4

WRONG
SIDE

In-Seam Pocket

The in-seam pocket may be cut in one with the front and back garment sections if using a lightweight fabric.

1 Draw the pocket freehand or 'dot' the shape onto the main pattern and trace off, **fig 1**.

2 If using a mediumweight fabric, cut the back pocket as an extension to the skirt pattern, **fig 1**, draw on the front pocket as above and cut away, **fig 2**. Remember to add seam allowance. Cut in lining fabric as this reduces bulk.

3 If using a heavy fabric, the front pocket pattern must be cut away on the seam line, **fig 2**, and cut in lining fabric. The back pocket should be cut with an extension from the seam line in the fashion fabric, **fig 3**. This prevents a 'gape' of lining showing when the pocket is used. The rest of the pocket is cut in lining fabric.

4 Tape the pocket fold line to prevent stretching, **fig 4**.

5 Join front and back pocket sections to their respective skirt pieces and, starting at the top of the garment, stitch down from the waist, round the pocket and on down the side seam.

The top of a pocket is normally parallel with the hipbone: do not make it too low. In-seam pockets are not suitable for close-fitting garments.

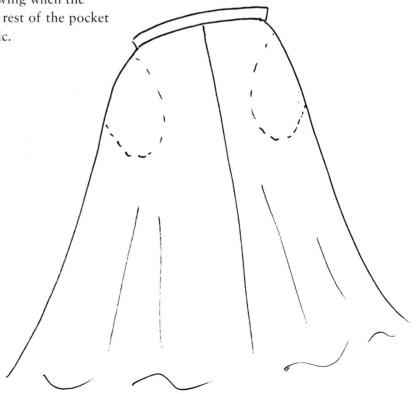

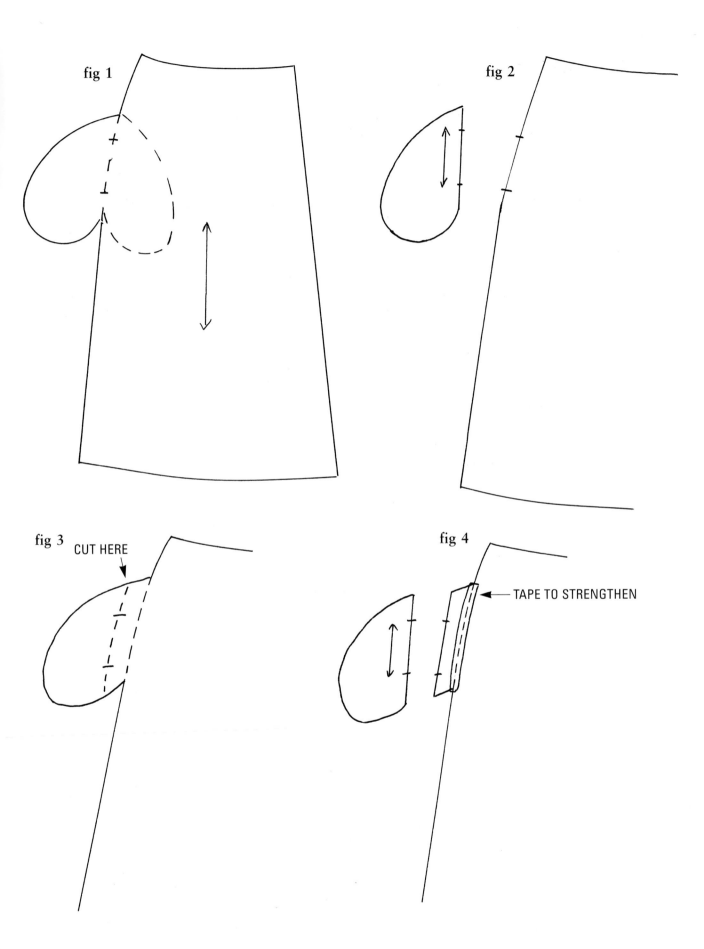

fig 1

fig 2

fig 3 CUT HERE

fig 4 TAPE TO STRENGTHEN

Bodice Pattern Cutting

Most bodice designs are achieved by dart manipulation or, in easy-fit fashions, by getting rid of the darts completely. However, it is vital to understand how darts work in order to cut patterns accurately.

Practise the following instructions before trying to cut bodice patterns.

1 Basic dart positions, **fig 1**, *must* always go to the bust point when pattern cutting. Thus, if the dart is shifted from above to below the bust, the point is still accurate.

2 To shift a dart, mark a line to the bust point for the new dart position. Slash open on this line to the point and fold out the original dart. The slashed opening is your new dart, **fig 2**.

3 All dart shaping may be transferred to one position, even if you start with two or three darts. Open a line for the new dart and close all others, **fig 3**. For dressmaker's dart, see dotted line.

4 There is much less dart adjustment on the back bodice, **fig 4**, except when cutting princess seams. For an easy dartless back, ignore the waist dart and, if the block has a shoulder dart, strike this out, straighten the shoulder line and shorten it by the length of the dart (see dotted line, **fig 5**). Final pattern, **fig 6**.

When pattern cutter's darts have been finalized, mark in dressmaker's darts. These should finish approximately 2.5 cm (1") short of the bust point.

The pattern *must* lie flat when old darts are folded out and new ones opened.

FRONT

fig 1

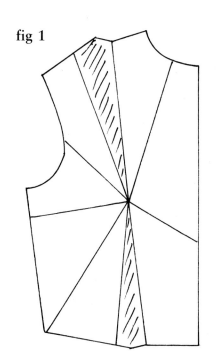

fig 2

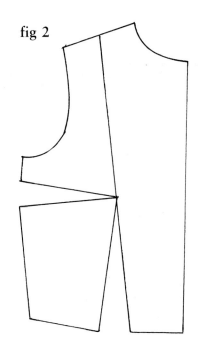

fig 3

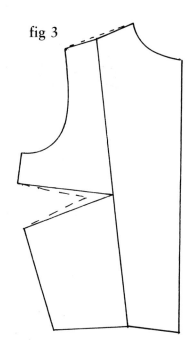

BACK

fig 4

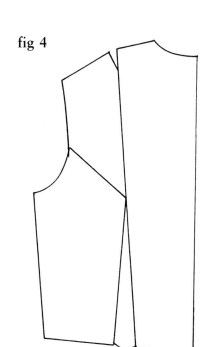

fig 5

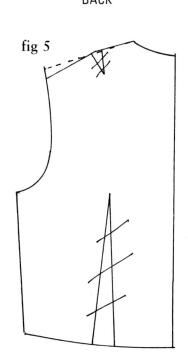

fig 6

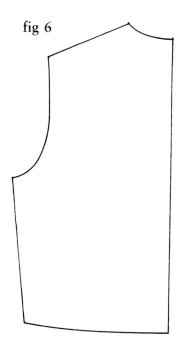

Fitted Bodice Block

Personal measurements should be used for a bodice block. Those shown here are for a standard size 12. Add ease to all horizontal measurements before starting.

1	Bust	88 cm + 5 or 6 cm ease (34 5/8" + 2" or 2 3/8" ease).
2	Waist	68 cm + 2.5 cm ease (26 3/4" + 1" ease).
3	Hip	93 cm + 5 cm ease (36 5/8" + 2" ease).
4	Cross back	34.4 cm + 2 cm ease (13 1/2" + 3/4" ease).
5	Cross chest	32.4 cm + 2 cm ease (12 3/4" + 3/4" ease).
6	Neck	38 cm + 2 cm ease (15" + 3/4" ease).
7	Total front dart	7 cm (2 3/4").
8	Centre front bodice	35 cm + 1 cm ease (13 3/4" + 3/8" ease).
9	Shoulder to waist	45 cm + 1 cm ease (17 3/4" + 3/8" ease).
10	Centre back bodice	40 cm + 2 cm ease (15 3/4" + 3/4" ease).
11	Back shoulder to waist	45 cm + 2 cm ease (17 3/4" + 3/4" ease).
12	Top arm length	54 cm + 2 cm ease (21 1/4 + 3/4" ease).
13	Elbow depth	20 cm + 2 cm ease (7 7/8" + 3/4" ease).
14	Shoulder length	12.25 cm + 1 cm ease (4 7/8" + 3/8" ease).
15	Armhole depth	21 cm + 2 cm ease (8 1/4" + 3/4" ease).

The hip measurement is needed for extending the bodice from waist to hip.

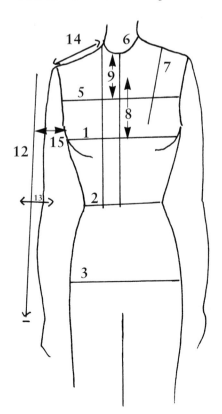
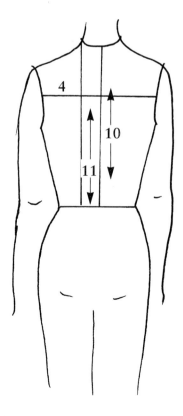

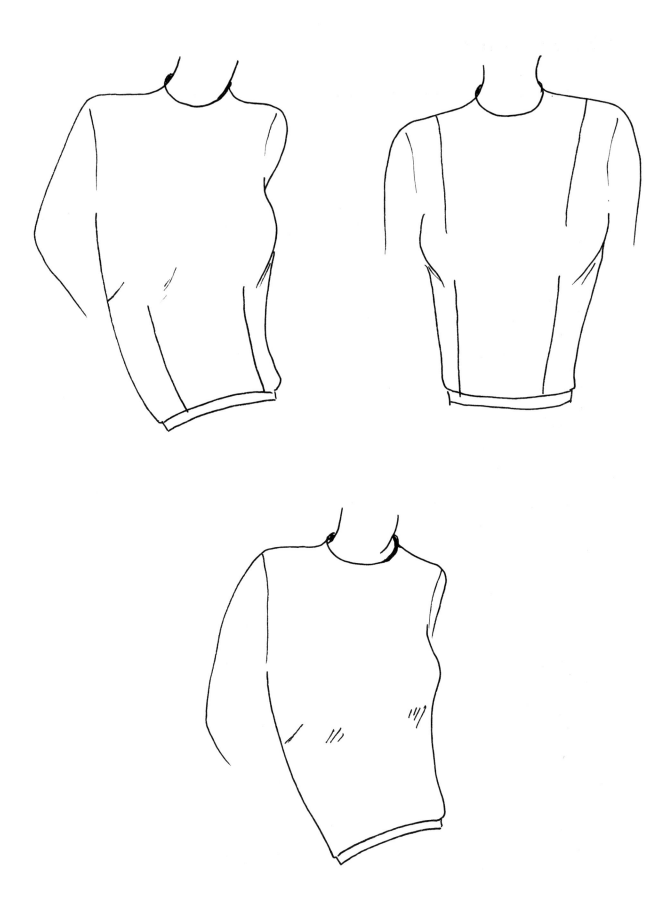

Bodice Draft

Back Bodice and Front Neck Shaping

0-1   Back shoulder to waist.

0-2   Half bust including ease.

2-3   Equals 0-1. Square down to 3 and across to 1.

0-4   2 cm (³/₄").

0-5   One fifth of neck.

4-5   Neck curve.

4-6   2.5 cm (1"). Square across 25 cm (9⁷/₈").

5-7   Shoulder length, measure from 5 onto line from 6.

7-8   Armhole depth. Square across both ways to 9 and 10.

9-10   Underarm line.

11   Half depth 7-8. Square out.

12   Half cross back measurement on line from 11.

2-13   One fifth neck measurement less 1 cm (³/₈").

2-14   Equals 2-13 + 1.5 cm (⁵/₈").

2-15   Equals 2-13 + 5 mm (¹/₄") diagonally from 2. Join 13-14-15 for neck curve.

16   Half of 1-3.

17   Squared up from 16 to line 9-10.

18-19   Half line 8-9 squared down.

For a semi-fitted back dart, mark a dart 1.5 cm (⁵/₈") either side of 19 and take off to nothing at 18.

Mark in the armhole from 7 to 12 to 17.

Front Bodice Shaping

Square across the block 20 cm (7⁷/₈") from 15.

13-20   Shoulder length + 4 cm (1⁵/₈") dart.

21   Half shoulder line 13-20.

22   4 cm (1⁵/₈") towards neckline from 21.

14-23   Bust point level, measure down from centre front neck (usually approximately 3 cm [1¹/₈"] below armhole).

24   Half measurement 10-14.

25   Square across from 24 to half cross chest measurement plus 2 cm for the dart on the line.

26   Square down from 25.

27   Half measurement of line 10-26 on line from 23. For the dart, rule back to 21 and 22 on the shoulder. Fold out the dart and correct shoulder line 13-20.

28   Square down from 27 and mark out 1.5 cm (⁵/₈") on each side for dart. Mark in armhole from 20-25-17.

Side Shaping

Mark out approximately 1.5 cm (⁵/₈") each side of 16 and draw back to nothing at underarm.

Mark up 1.5 cm (⁵/₈") from 16 and curve back to front and back darts for the waist shaping.

For sleeveless styles raise the underarm by approximately 1.5 cm (⁵/₈") to prevent gape.

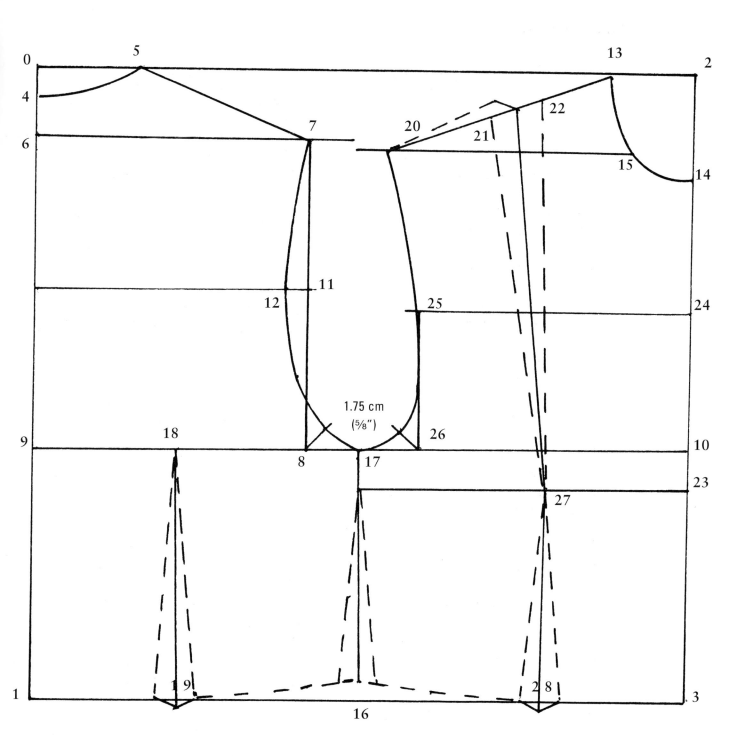

Loose-Fitting Bodice Block

The fitted bodice block can be amended for looser styles.

1 Shift the front shoulder dart to the side seam (see p37).

2 Fold dart out with the bulk going down the bodice. Draw in the correct line.

3 Draw a vertical line from the side seam point of the new dart (see dotted lines).

4 Extend the underarm curve to meet this line. Measure the amount of extension.

5 Extend the cross chest line by the same amount as at underarm and redraw the armhole curve (see dotted line).

6 For a looser armhole, drop the curve by 1.5-2 cm (5/8-3/4"). Remember that the sleeve head must be adjusted to match. Slash down the front and back arm lines and spread (see pp78-9). Redraw the sleeve head.

7 Add the same amount to the cross back line and side seam on the back bodice as at the front, lowering the armhole to match. Draw a line back to shoulder point (see dotted lines).

8 Use a small waist/bust dart for a gentle fit.

Dartless Bodice

For a very easy, dartless shape, slash from hem to shoulder on back and front and spread the pieces evenly by 1 cm (3/8"), or more if wanted. Ignore the dart.

Sleeve for Dartless Bodice

If the bodice armhole is made larger for easy-fit garments then the sleeve head must be widened. The sports sleeve (pp96-7) is useful in easy bodice styles.

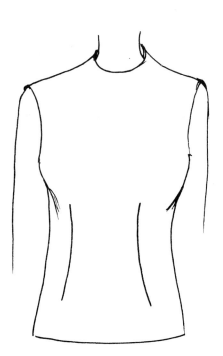

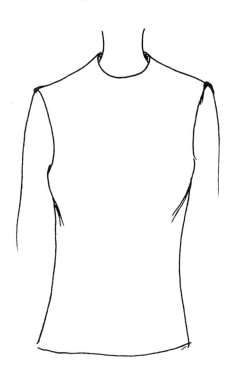

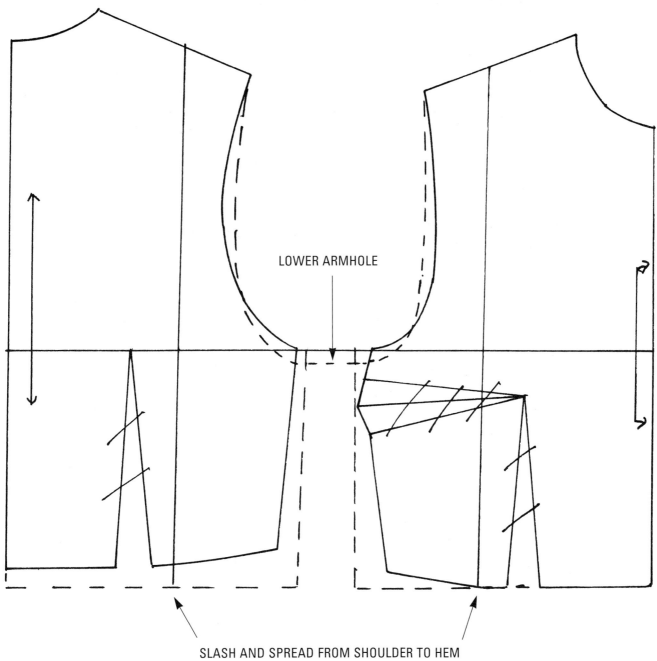

LOWER ARMHOLE

SLASH AND SPREAD FROM SHOULDER TO HEM
FOR ADDITIONAL EASE

Buttonstands and Facings

Buttonstands

1 Decide on the size of the buttons and add a buttonstand of the same width to the bodice pattern, **fig 1.**

2 Place the first button parallel with the bust point (to prevent gape) and space evenly from there, **fig 2.**

3 Buttonholes should be the size of the button plus about a quarter. Thus, a 1 cm (3/8") button needs a hole of 1.25 cm (1/2"). This should be a little larger if using a very bulky button. About a quarter of the buttonhole should be over the centre front line, with the remaining three-quarters over the stand. This centres the button on the centre front line, **fig 2.**

Facings

1 Complete the bodice pattern and draw in the facings (see dotted line), **fig 3.**

2 Trace off the facing section and cut it as a separate pattern piece, **fig 4.**

3 Ensure that back and front facings marry accurately at the shoulder seam.

Straight grain on facings are as for the garment.

fig 1

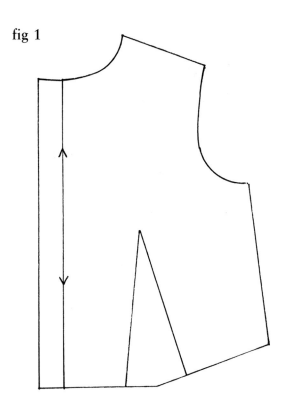

fig 2

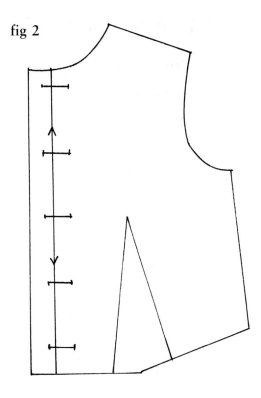

fig 3

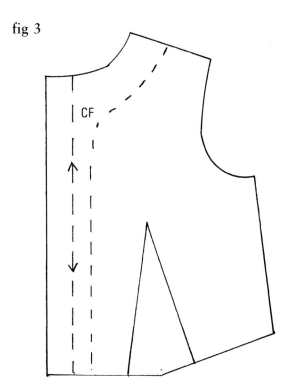

fig 4

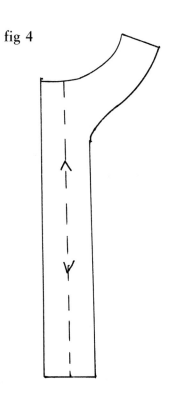

Bodice with Yoke

This is a comfortable, easy-fit feature popular in shirts and blouses.
Use a bodice block with shoulder and waist dart.

1 Outline the front block. Ignore the waist dart; this will be used for fullness, **fig 1**.

2 Draw in the yoke style line and put in balance marks.

3 Cut away the yoke section and close out dart. Soften the angle made by removing the dart (see dotted line), **fig 2**.

4 Ignore the lower part of the shoulder dart; this forms fullness for gathering.

5 Redraw both pattern pieces, **fig 3**.

6 Outline the back block. If using a fitted block with a shoulder dart, this must be removed as follows.

7 First, mark a line from the base of the shoulder dart to the point of the lower dart and draw in yoke line, **fig 4**. Put in balance marks.

8 Cut away yoke, cut up line to the base of the dart and fold this out, **fig 5**. Adjust width at the armhole edge to compensate for the extra width created below the dart fold (see dotted line), **fig 5**.

9 On the lower section of the back, slash through the centre of dart and up to the top of the line. Spread for fullness, **fig 5**.

10 Redraw, marking the position of the gathers, **fig 6**.

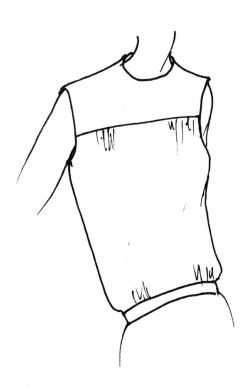

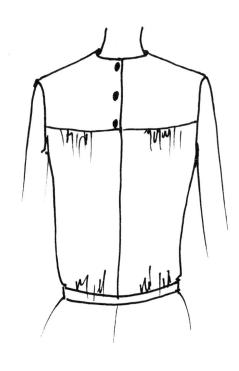

FRONT

fig 1

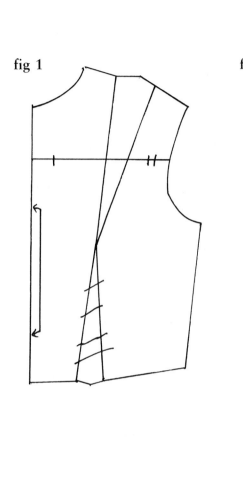

fig 2

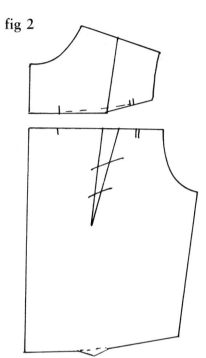

fig 3

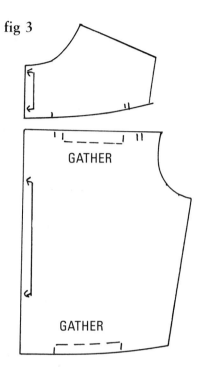

GATHER

GATHER

BACK

fig 4

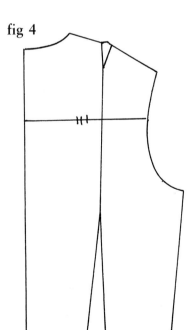

fig 5

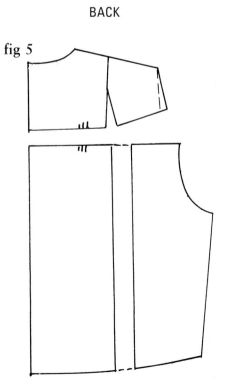

fig 6

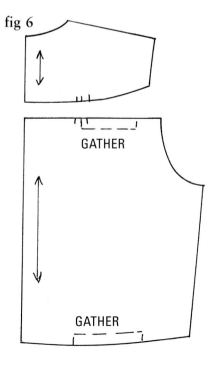

GATHER

GATHER

Basque Waist Bodice

A very fitted shape emphasizes a small waist and can disguise
a small bust.

1 Shift all the dart to the waist/bust line and
draw in style line and balance marks, **fig 1**.

2 Cut away the lower section and fold out
all dart shaping. Soften the angles
formed by folding (see dotted line), **fig 2**.

3 The small dart left in the upper bodice
may be used for soft gathering or
pleating, (illustration 1).

4 For a fuller upper bodice, draw in vertical
slash lines, **fig 4**, and slash and spread
up to, but not through, the shoulder, **fig 5**.

5 Redraw and mark gathering across area
that has been spread, (illustration 2).

The back of the pattern may be shaped
as wanted but must marry with the front
at the side seam. It is more flattering to
curve the style line down slightly at the
centre back.

Do not add too much fullness on the upper
back bodice. It can create the appearance
of round shoulders.

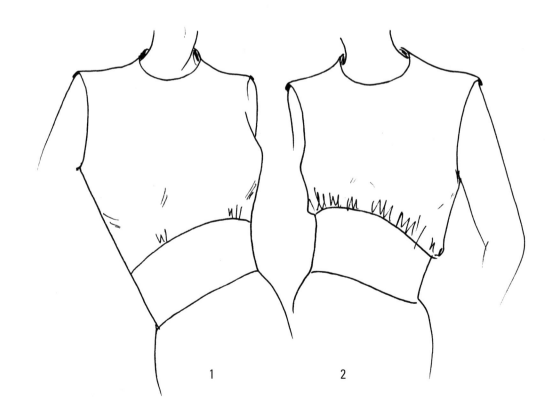

1   2

fig 1

fig 2

fig 3

GATHER

fig 4

fig 5

fig 6

GATHER

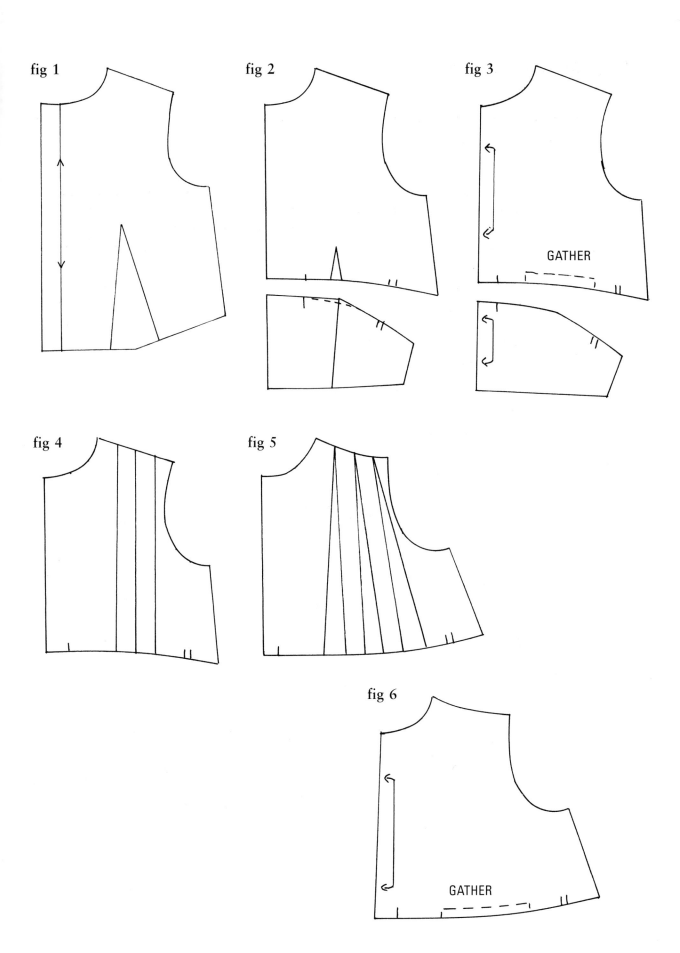

Pleated Front Bodice

This style flatters most figures, except perhaps the very thin, as the vertical lines tend to have a slimming effect.

1 This style is easier to achieve with a dartless block. For a figure with a large bust, where some dart shaping may be needed, use a shoulder dart and distribute the dart allowance evenly between the pleats.

2 Outline the block and mark in pleat lines from shoulder to hem. Number the pieces. Draw a horizontal line across, **fig 1**.

3 Slash through the pleat lines. Mark a horizontal line on a new piece of paper and spread the pattern pieces, matching the horizontal lines to ensure accuracy, **fig 2**. Redraw, marking in the pleats.

4 Fold out the pleats before recutting. This gives the correct shape at the top of the pleats, **fig 3**.

If using a centre front opening with this style, combine the pleated front with a fly front opening (see pp64-5)

fig 1

fig 2

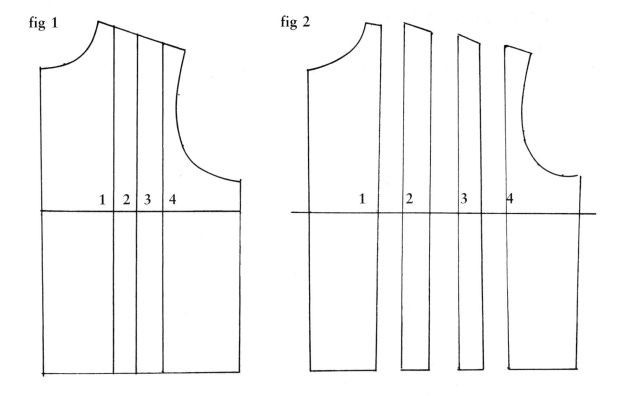

fig 3

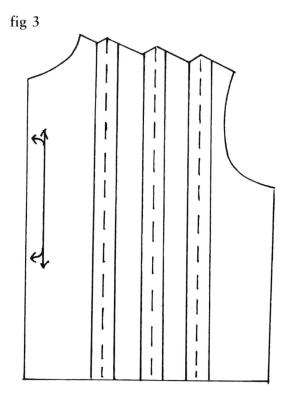

Princess Line Bodice

The continuous vertical seaming of the princess line gives a slimming effect. Style lines must marry on the shoulder for the shoulder to hem version.

Princess Line 1: Shoulder to Hem Seam

1 Use a block with shoulder and waist darts, **fig 1**.

2 Put in balance marks across the full width of both darts, **fig 1**.

3 Cut away the darts and through the bust point, **fig 2**. For an easy fit, use only half of the waist/bust dart, **fig 2**.

4 Soften the angles through the bust point, (see dotted line).

5 The straight grain is at the centre front (and centre back) and at the centre of the side panels, **fig 3**.

Princess Line 2: Curved into Armhole

1 Draw in a style line from the armhole and through the bust point, **fig 4**. Put in balance marks.

2 Cut away on the style line and through the bust point.

3 Fold out the shoulder dart, **fig 5**.

4 Cut away the waist dart (or half of it for an easier fit), **fig 5**. Soften the shaping if necessary (see dotted line) and redraw, **fig 6**. The bust curve may need easing onto the straighter edge.

5 Straight grain is as for Princess Line 1.

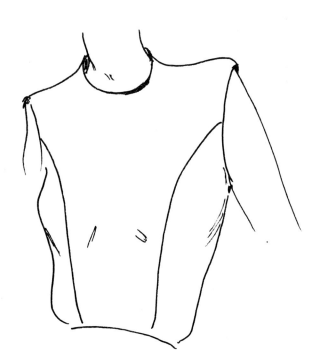

PRINCESS LINE 1

fig 1   fig 2   fig 3

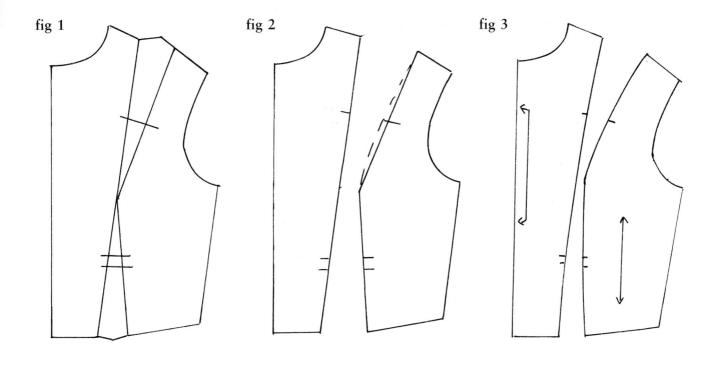

PRINCESS LINE 2

fig 4   fig 5   fig 6

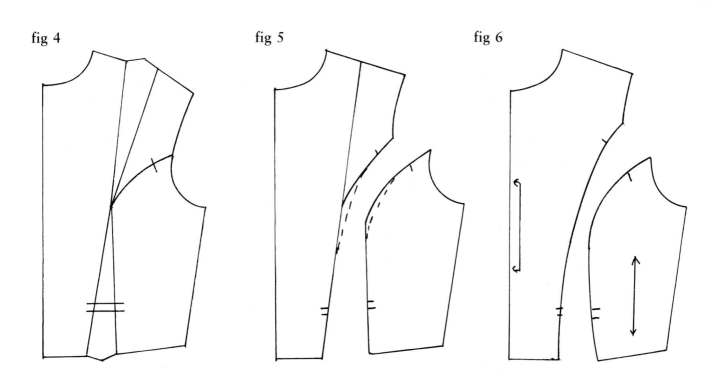

Crossover Bodice

This style emphasizes the ratio between bust and waist.

1 Outline the whole bodice, **fig 1**. The 'crossover' usually lies from the right shoulder/neck point to the base of the left waist dartline.

2 Lower the neckline as much as the style requires and draw in the style line, **fig 1**.

3 Cut away on this line and mark in two lines from the bust point to the new neckline, one above and one below the bust, **fig 2**.

4 Slash open the waist dart to the bust point and fold out by approximately 5 mm ($^1/4$") on each line from the bust to neckline, **fig 3**. This shortens the neck edge and prevents the neckline gaping. Redraw (see dotted line), **fig 3**.

5 You now have an enormous underbust/waist dart. Reduce this (see dotted line), and shave off at the side seam to correct, **fig 3**.

6 Final pattern, **fig 4**.

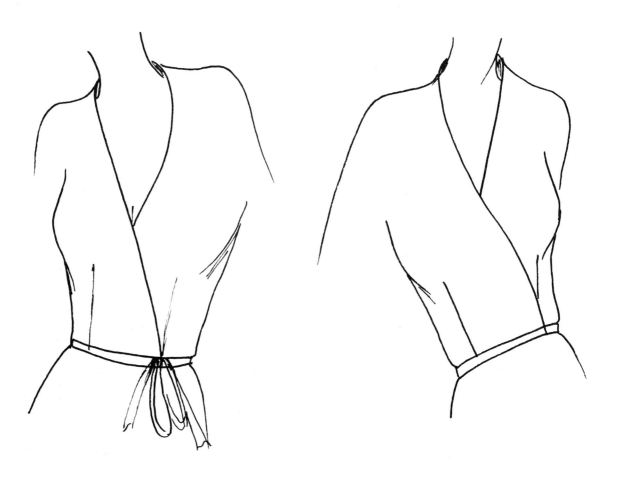

fig 1

fig 2

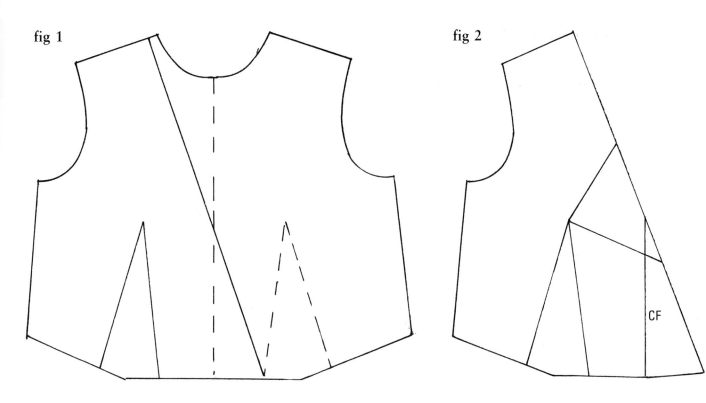

fig 3

fig 4

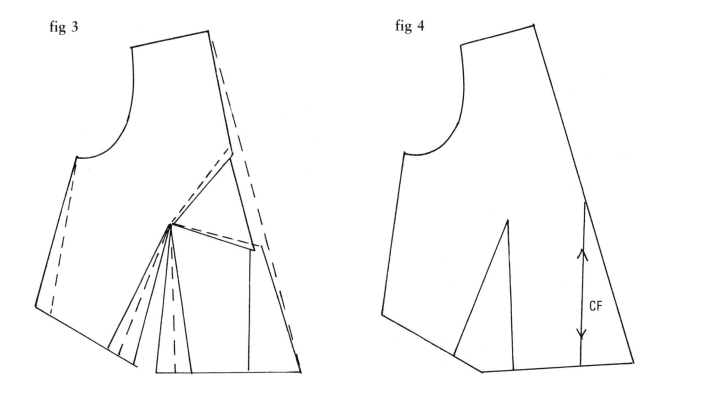

Bodice with Asymmetric Opening

This is an alternative to the double-breasted style without the bulk of the extra wrap in the front.

1 Working on a complete front with waist darts, draw a line from the left bust point to the centre shoulder, **fig 1**.

2 Cut through this line, cutting away the dart (or half of the dart for an easy fit), **fig 2**. Mark the straight grain on the centre front and at the centre of the side panel and soften the angle at the bust point, **fig 2**.

3 Add a buttonstand to each section, **fig 3**. Face the shoulder and the corresponding buttonstand to the back shoulder.

This style is attractive combined with princess seaming but, if darts are used, these should complement the opening line.

This bodice can be worn with a tie at the waist. This is achieved by attaching bias strips, stitched into tubes, to the waist edge and slotting them through from the underside at the waist seam.

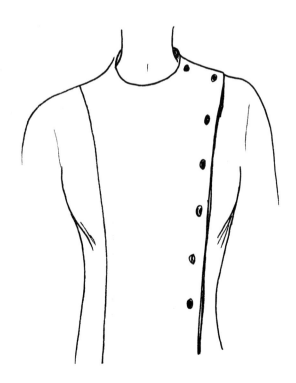

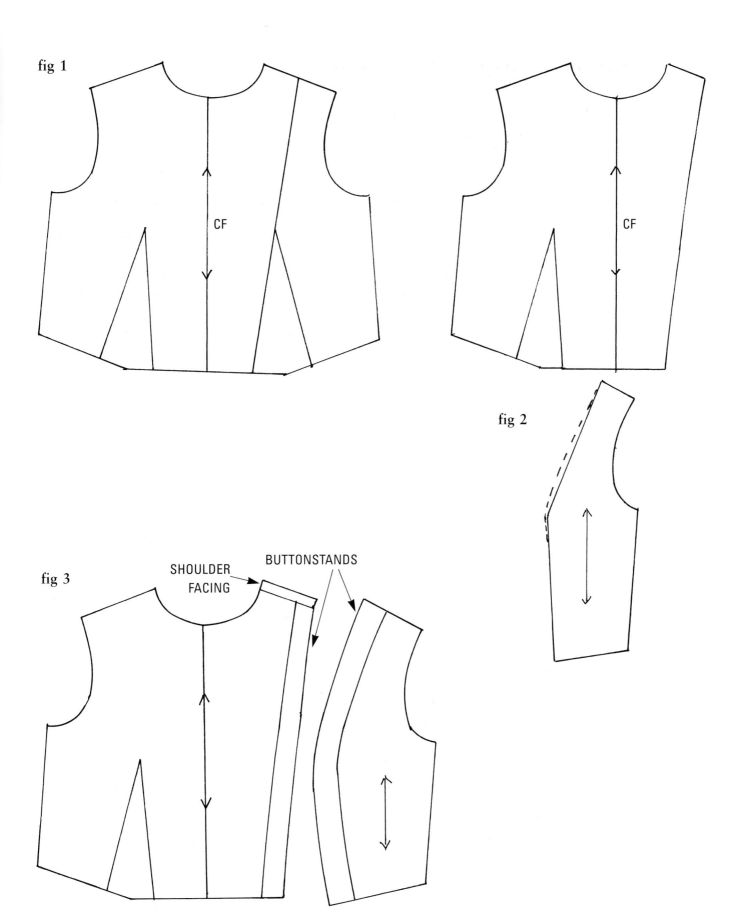

fig 1

CF

CF

fig 2

fig 3

SHOULDER FACING

BUTTONSTANDS

Double Breasted Opening

This opening is most commonly used on a jacket or overblouse shape.

1 Outline a full front block, decide on the double breasted line and draw in, **fig 1**. The opening should line up with the waist dart on the left front.

2 Draw in a break line for the rever from shoulder to centre front, **fig 1**. Cut away.

3 Mark a line to the neck edge from the bust point. Slash open the waist dart to the bust point. Shorten the neck edge by folding out by approximately 1 cm (3/8") on the neck edge line, **fig 2**.

4 Draw in the correct neckline (see dotted line), **fig 2**.

5 Add a buttonstand to the opening and draw the rever shape onto the pattern, **fig 3**.

6 Measure the extra width created by slashing the dart and remove the same amount at the side seam. Reduce the dart, (see dotted line), **fig 3**. Lower the side bust dart by marking in a new line and slashing it open. Close the original dart, **fig 3**.

7 Trace off the collar shape and place against the neck edge, **fig 4**.

8 Facings must go across the left and right fronts to accommodate the buttonholes, **fig 4**.

Care must be taken in selecting fabric for this style as it can be very bulky if a heavy material is used. It is good and warm for coats and jackets.

fig 1

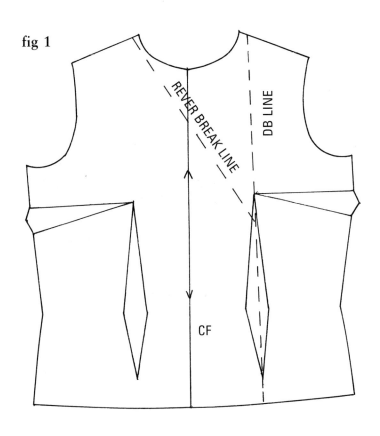

fig 2

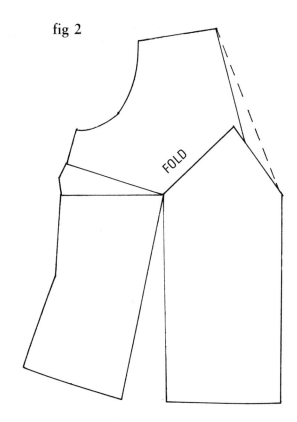

fig 3

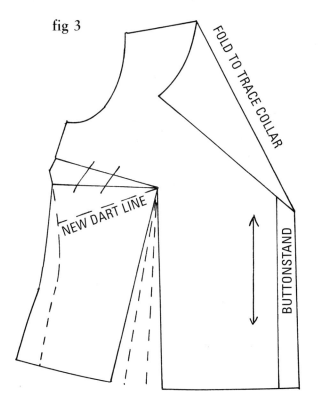

fig 4

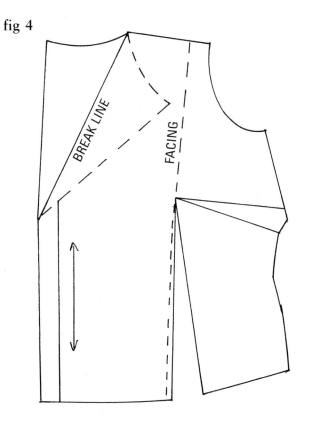

Deep Cowl Neckline

This style was very popular in the 1930s when bias cutting first became fashionable. If properly cut it is very flattering.

1 Outline the block and lower the neck as wanted. Draw in curves for the cowl from the centre front to the shoulder, **fig 1**.

2 Slash from the centre front along the curves up to, but not through, the shoulder and close out the darts, **fig 2**.

3 Place the centre front against the fold of a piece of paper, folding along the top of pattern, **fig 2**. This gives an integral facing. Redraw.

4 Open out the pattern for the whole front and mark the centre front and the true bias line, **fig 3**.

5 If a looser style is wanted, do not remove the waist dart but use for fullness. Square down from armhole.

A cowl neck is equally attractive on the back and front of a garment.

A soft jersey fabric need not be cut on the bias but in any woven fabric, however soft, the drape will hang correctly only if it is cut on the bias. The back bodice should be cut on the straight grain.

Small weights may be needed inside the drapes to hold them in position.

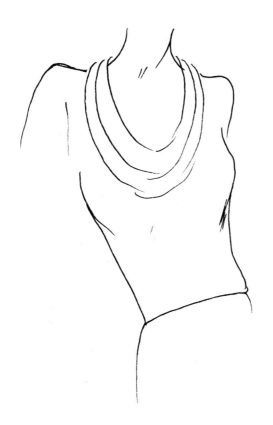

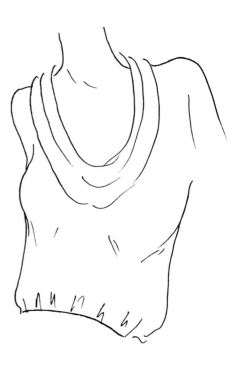

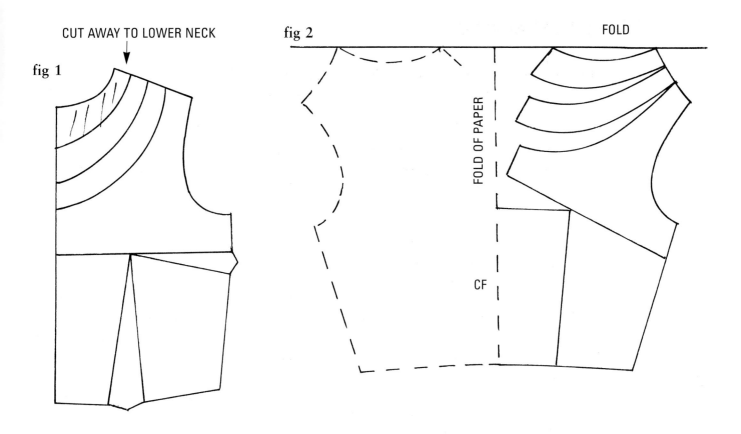

fig 1

CUT AWAY TO LOWER NECK

fig 2

FOLD

FOLD OF PAPER

CF

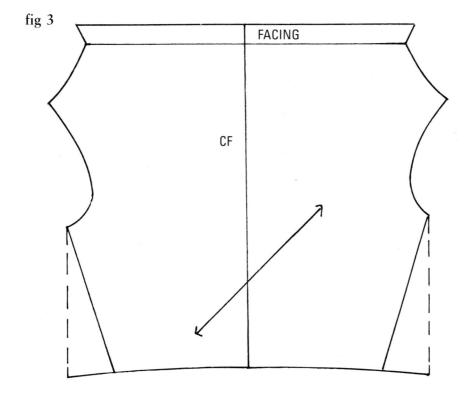

fig 3

FACING

CF

High Cut Cowl

The high-cut cowl has a tailored appearance. Though shown here with the whole bodice cut on the bias, it is possible to cut it as a bias inset on a straight-cut bodice (see dotted line, sketch below). A soft crepe or similar weight material should be used for this.

1 Trace off a whole front from the block and move all dart shaping to the waist/bust line. Mark in the centre front and draw a line connecting the darts at the bust point, **fig 1**.

2 Slash open down the centre front to the bust line and across to the bust points. Fold out the darts, **fig 2**.

3 Draw a straight line across from one shoulder point to the other, **fig 2**, and trace off the facing, **fig 3**. The straight grain is on the true bias.

4 For an easy fit, square down from the armhole to the waist, **fig 3**.

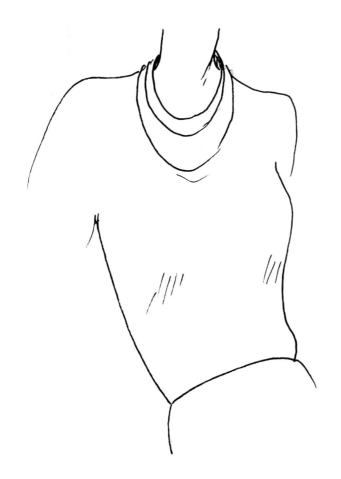

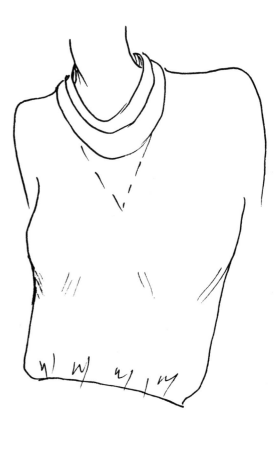

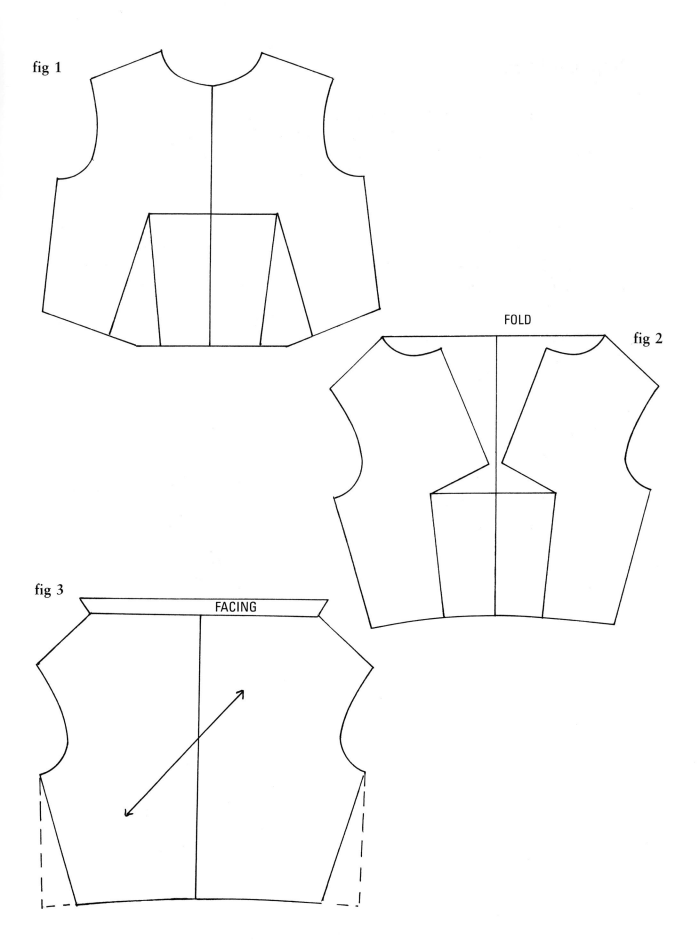

fig 1

fig 2

FOLD

fig 3

FACING

Fly Front Opening

This detail conceals a front opening and is often used with a vertically pleated front, the fly giving the impression of an additional pleat.

1 Outline the block, usually a dartless or side bust dart block. Add the buttonstand and mark a strip the same width as the buttonstand the other side of the centre front (see dotted line), **fig 1**.

2 Add the facing which should be the same width as the distance from the dotted line to the edge of the buttonstand, **fig 1**.

3 For the fly front, measure the width from the dotted line to the outer edge of the facing and add this distance to the edge of the facing, **fig 2**.

4 Fold out the fly front to cut the neck edge of the pattern correctly.

5 If working with a narrow piece of fabric, the fly front may be cut separately, **fig 3**.

It is best to use a fairly soft fabric as too crisp a finish will make the pleats stand away from the body.

fig 1

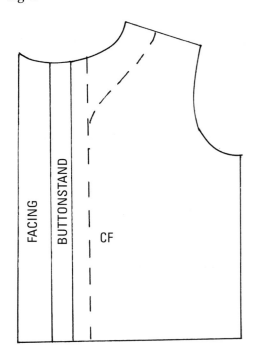

fig 2

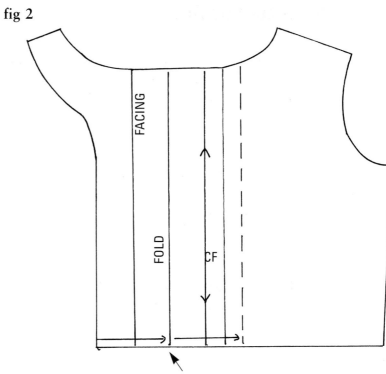

FOLD TO DOTTED LINE

fig 3

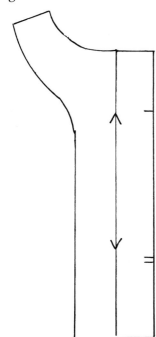

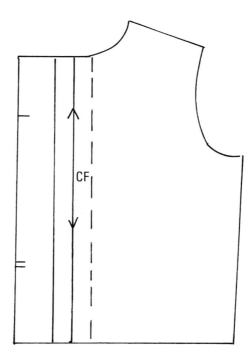

Necklines and Facings

Cutting a neckline means cutting into an area which includes a certain amount of ease. This can create an unsightly gape unless corrected during cutting: it is important to shorten the neck edge.

Square Neck

1 On these styles, the horizontal and vertical sections of the neckline must be shortened.

2 Draw in the neckline and mark a line from the bust point to the horizontal neck edge, **fig 1**.

3 Cut away on style line, slash the dart open to point and fold out about 5 mm from bust point to neck. Correct the neckline (see dotted line), **fig 2**.

4 To adjust the vertical section of the neckline, straighten the shoulder edge, **fig 2**.

5 Mark in the facings and trace off, **fig 3**.

Sweetheart Neck

Follow the instructions for the square neck, referring to **figs 4, 5, 6**.

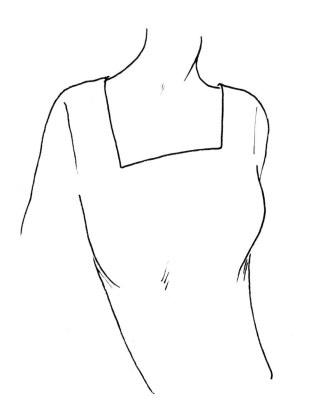
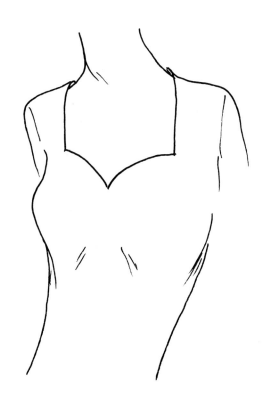

SQUARE NECK

fig 1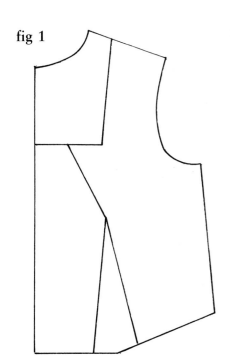

fig 2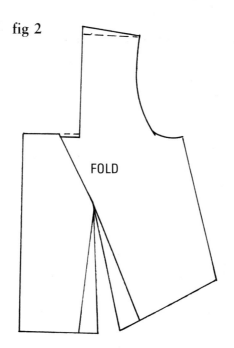

FOLD

fig 3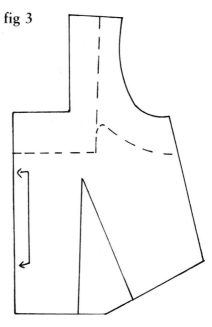

SWEETHEART NECK

fig 4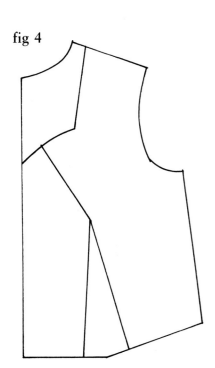

fig 5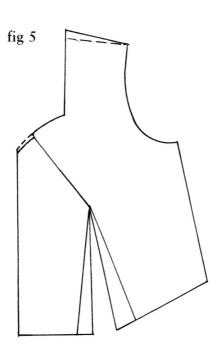

fig 6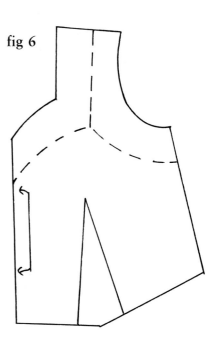

V-Neck

1 Outline the block and draw in the neckline. Mark a line from the bust point to the neck edge, **fig 1**. Cut away on the style line.

2 Slash up the existing dart to bust point and fold out approximately 5 mm (¹/₄") at the neck edge, **fig 2**. For large busts take out 1 cm (³/₈"). Straighten the neck edge.

3 Remove the width added by slashing the dart by narrowing the pattern at the side seam (see dotted line), **fig 3**.

4 Mark in facings and trace off. The neck and armhole facing may be cut in one, **fig 3**.

Scoop Neck

1 Work as for V-Neck but, if cutting a deep scoop, shorten the neck edge in two places, **fig 4**. Open the dart to the bust point and close out by about 5 mm (¹/₄") on each line to the neck edge.

2 Correct the neckline, **fig 5**

3 Trace off facings and reduce pattern at dart and side seam, **fig 6**.

4 Reduce the dart to its original width, **fig 6**.

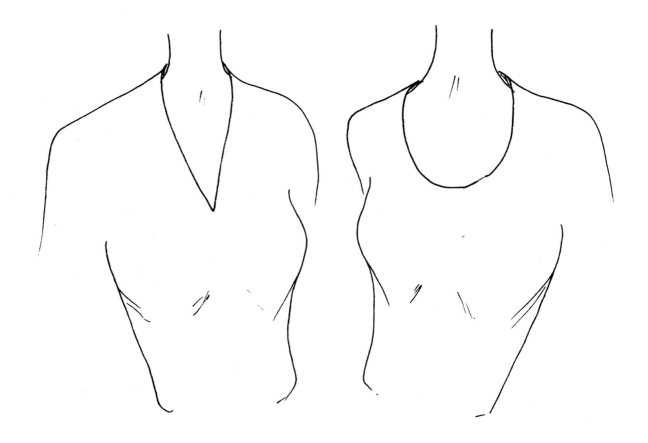

V-NECK

fig 1

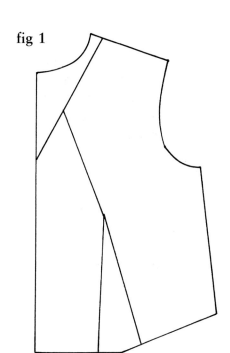

fig 2

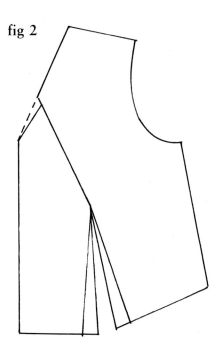

fig 3

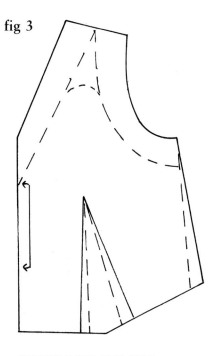

REDUCE DART AND SIDE
SEAM TO DOTTED LINE

SCOOP NECK

fig 4

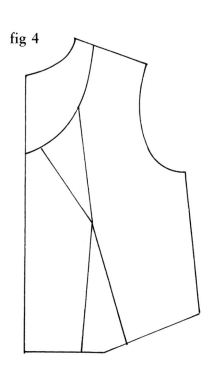

fig 5

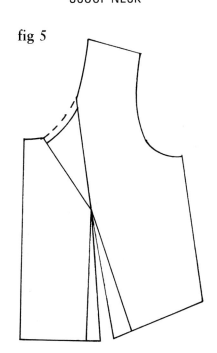

fig 6

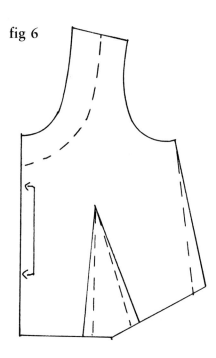

Collars

The two collar types most commonly used in dress patterns are the straightband collar, cut on a straight line the length of the garment neck edge, and the Peter Pan collar, cut to the shape of the garment neck edge. The shawl or grown-on collar has been traditionally used in tailoring, but in recent years has become increasingly popular in lighter clothing. All collars have a 'stand' which is seamed to the garment and stands against the neck of the wearer and (other than the mandarin collar) a 'fall' which drops down from the top of the stand and covers the neck seam.

Straightband Collar

1 The collar is cut in one piece, incorporating the stand and fall. The straight grain is at the centre back or the fold line.

2 Place the front and back garment patterns together at the shoulder and measure the neck edge, **fig 1**. Draw a straight line this length on folded paper.

3 Draw the required collar shape on the line against the fold, **fig 2**. The collar fall must be slightly longer than the stand in order to cover the neck seam, **fig 3**.

4 Cut out the pattern on the fold and open out. The fold marks the straight grain, **fig 4**. Mark the pattern 'cut 2'.

5 Join to the neck edge, **fig 5**.

6 The collar design may go to the centre front or to the edge of buttonstand. Adjust the collar length as required.

Mandarin or Stand Collar

1 Follow the instructions for straightband collar from points 2 to 5, **figs 1, 2**. Shape the front edge. The sketches below show some design ideas.

2 Working this way the collar will stand slightly away from the neck, sketch 2, **fig 6**.

3 For the collar to stand close to the neck, sketch 3, adjustments must be made. Draw out the collar as above and then divide it into equal sections, **fig 7**. Fold out at the upper edge by approximately 5 mm on each line, **fig 8**.

5 Redraw the collar and cut 2, **fig 9**.

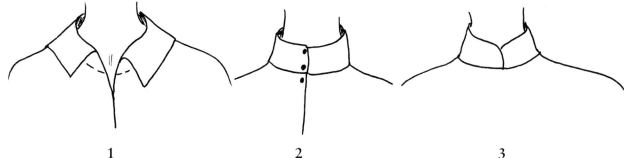

1   2   3

STRAIGHTBAND COLLAR

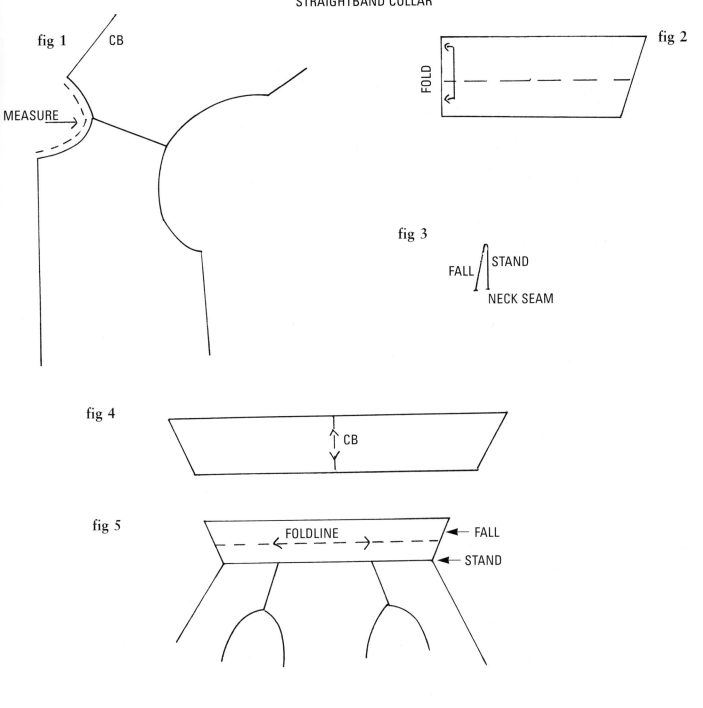

fig 1 CB

MEASURE

FOLD fig 2

fig 3

FALL STAND

NECK SEAM

fig 4 CB

fig 5 FOLDLINE FALL

STAND

MANDARIN COLLAR

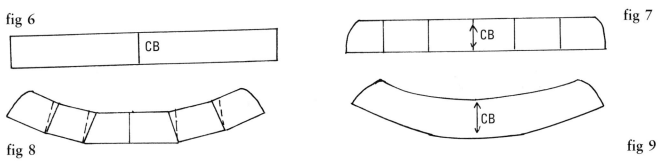

fig 6 CB

fig 7 CB

fig 8

fig 9 CB

Peter Pan Collar

'Peter Pan' is a generic term for collars cut to the neck edge shape of the garment. The front and back bodice should meet at the neck edge on the shoulder to draw the shape. The outer edges of the shoulder (adjacent to the sleeve head) must overlap a little to give a slight 'stand' and prevent the seam from showing at the neck edge.

1 Place the bodice back and front pattern together at the shoulder, overlapping slightly at the armhole edge, **fig 1**.

2 Draw the collar onto the neck, **fig 1**, shape and trace off, **fig 2**. Cut 2. The straight grain is at either the centre front or centre back.

Sailor Collar

1 Cut the neck line away, following the instructions for the V-Neck (p68).

2 Follow the instructions for the Peter Pan collar, **fig 3**, with the bodice pattern pieces meeting and overlapping at neck and shoulder points.

3 Draw the collar onto the pattern and trace off with the straight grain to the centre back, **fig 4**. Cut 2.

PETER PAN COLLAR

fig 1

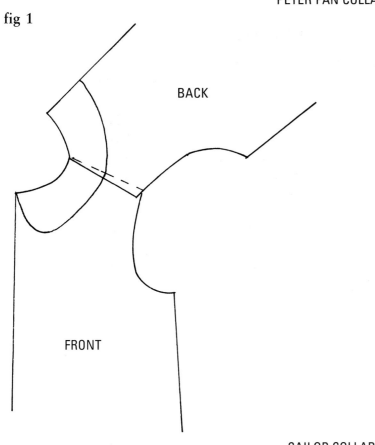

BACK

FRONT

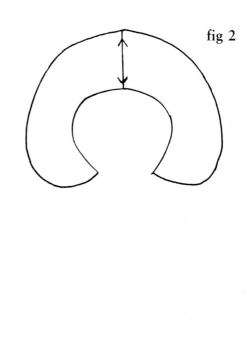

fig 2

SAILOR COLLAR

fig 3

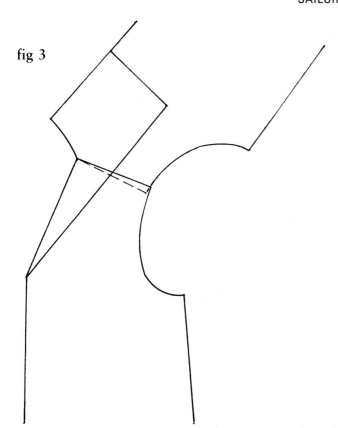

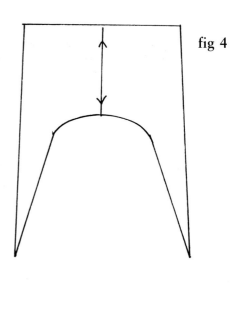

fig 4

Two-Piece Shirt Collar

This collar is similar in appearance to a straightband collar but is more tailored. The stand and fall are cut separately to give a better fit and the stand is shaped to the neck.

Men's shirt collars are normally cut by this method.

1 Measure the neck including the buttonstand, **fig 1**.

2 Cut the collar stand, following the instructions for the fitted mandarin collar (p70). Mark the centre front line at each end of the section, **fig 2**.

3 Measure along the upper edge between the centre front lines and draw a straight line to this length.

4 Draw the straight collar fall on this line, following the instructions for the straightband collar (p70) but only to the depth of the collar fall, **fig 3**.

5 Make up as in **fig 4**.

fig 1

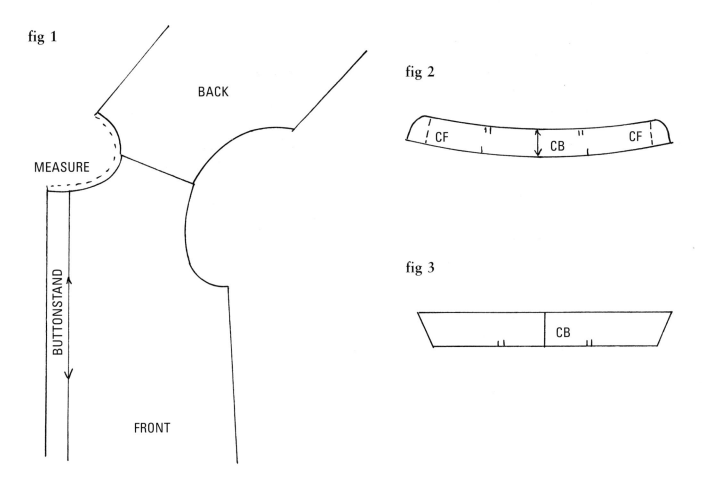

fig 2

fig 3

fig 4

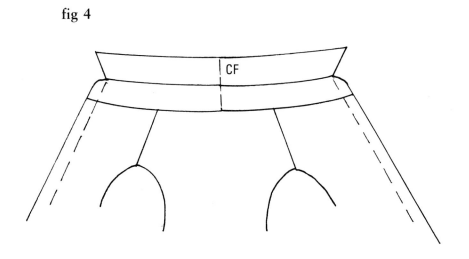

Shawl or 'Grown On' Collar

This collar is more usually seen on outerwear, though during the 1940s it was used for 'neat' collar styles, conforming with the limited use of fabric allowed under rationing. The shawl collar is now also seen on dresses and blouses.

1 Outline block. For a dress, lower the neck slightly at the shoulder, **fig 1**. For outerwear, raise the neck slightly, by no more than 1 cm (³/₈").

2 Draw in the neckline and follow the instructions for the V-Neck to prevent gape (pp68-9), **fig 1**.

3 Add buttonstand, **fig 1**.

4 Extend the neckline above the shoulder by the length of the back neck pattern and draw on the collar shape, **fig 1**. This collar includes both stand and fall, so must be deep enough for both.

5 For a softer, flatter collar the outer edge must be lengthened. Mark 2 or 3 lines evenly spaced along back section, **fig 2**, and slash and spread, **fig 3**.

6 Redraw, marking in the breakline and facings. Trace off the facings and collar, **fig 4**.

7 The undercollar remains cut in one with the garment, the top collar is cut in one with the facings. Refer to a dressmakers' manual for making up instructions.

fig 1

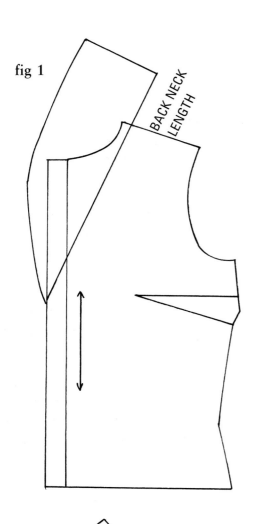

BACK NECK LENGTH

fig 2

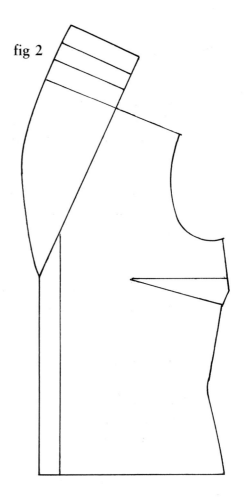

fig 3

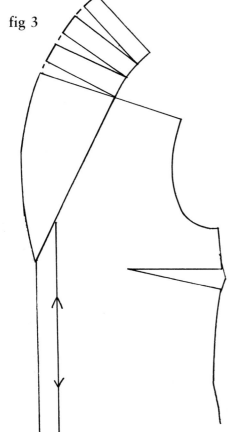

fig 4

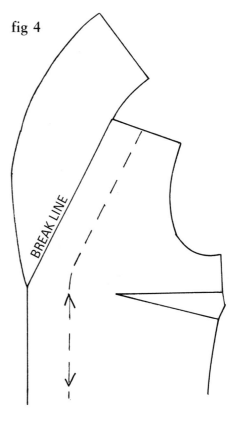

BREAK LINE

Sleeve Pattern Cutting

All set-in sleeves have some ease in the head; that is, the sleeve head measures more than the bodice armhole. This allows room for the arm to pivot without tearing the garment. If the difference is more than about 2-3 cm ($\frac{3}{4}$-$1\frac{1}{8}$") (depending on the stiffness of the fabric), it may be difficult to insert the sleeve smoothly.

Take care not to ease under the arm as this creates bulk where it is uncomfortable and unsightly. Nor should the very top of the head be eased as this is the straight grain and more difficult to compress. Easing is done up the slope at the back and front of the head where it is cut off-grain. Here, the fabric is easily manipulated and the garment takes more pull from arm movement (see dotted lines opposite).

The straight sleeve is the basic shape from which all others are derived. If using this without further alteration, a slight curve must be added to the hem at the back arm line to allow elbow room and the same amount removed at the front to reduce bulk when arm is bent, **fig 1**.

Sleeve Fitting Lines

1 Mark in the top arm line down the centre of the sleeve and the front and back arm lines halfway between the top arm line and the seam, **fig 2**.

2 Mark the elbow line so that it is parallel with the waistline when the underarm is lined up with the bodice, **fig 2**.

3 Mark in other horizontal lines halfway between the elbow and underarm and the elbow and wrist, **fig 2**.

4 Fold in on front and back arm lines to the top line. Seam lines should meet evenly, **fig 3**.

Straight grain on sleeves, unless otherwise shown, is down the top arm line.

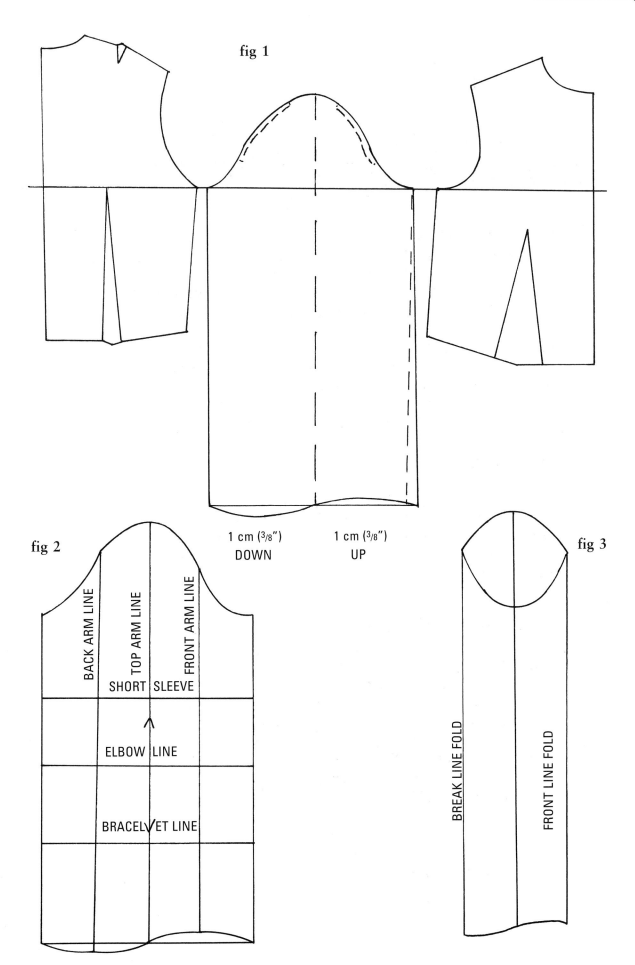

fig 1

1 cm (³/₈")
DOWN

1 cm (³/₈")
UP

fig 2

BACK ARM LINE

TOP ARM LINE

FRONT ARM LINE

SHORT SLEEVE

ELBOW LINE

BRACELET LINE

fig 3

BREAK LINE FOLD

FRONT LINE FOLD

Sleeve Block

1 Trace off the armhole and side seam from the bodice block. Extend the side seam up to 2 cm (¾") below the level of the front shoulder. Mark the underarm line. This becomes the top arm line.

2 Underarm at side seam.

3 Cross back line (trace from bodice block).

4 Cross chest line (trace from bodice block).

5 Back shoulder point.

6 Front shoulder point.

1-7 Equals distance 3-5 + 5 mm (¼").

1-8 Equals 4-6 + 1.2 cm (½").

7-9 Equals 2-3 + 1.3 cm (½").

8-10 2-4 + 5 mm (¼").

Curve for armhole shaping, following the measurements shown on the diagram below. Square down from 9 and 10 to the extent of the sleeve length.

Mark in the front and back arm lines halfway between the seam and top arm line.

Shape the hem curve for elbow room as shown below.

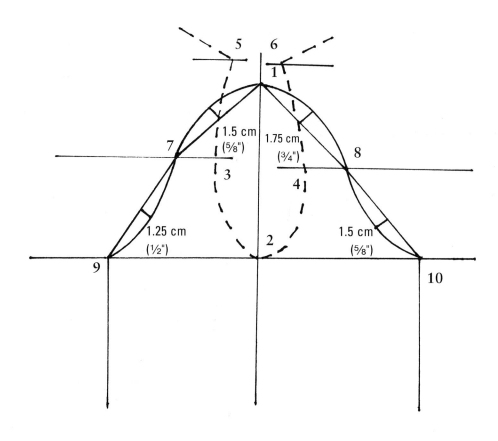

Semi-Fitted Sleeve Block

1 Outline the basic sleeve and square off at the wrist. Take off about 4 cm (1⅝") at the front and back wrist and rule back to nothing at the underarm, **fig 1**.

2 Re-mark the front and back arm lines halfway between the top arm line and the new seam lines, **fig 1**.

3 Slash across the elbow line from the back seam to the centre and fold out the top arm line from wrist to elbow, **fig 2**. This opens up the elbow dart.

4 Redraw the sleeve with the front and back arm lines halfway between the seam and top arm line and curve the hem down by 1 cm (⅜") at the back and up 1 cm (⅜") at front, **fig 3**.

5 The dart is stitched only to the back arm line, thus giving the greatest fullness over the elbow.

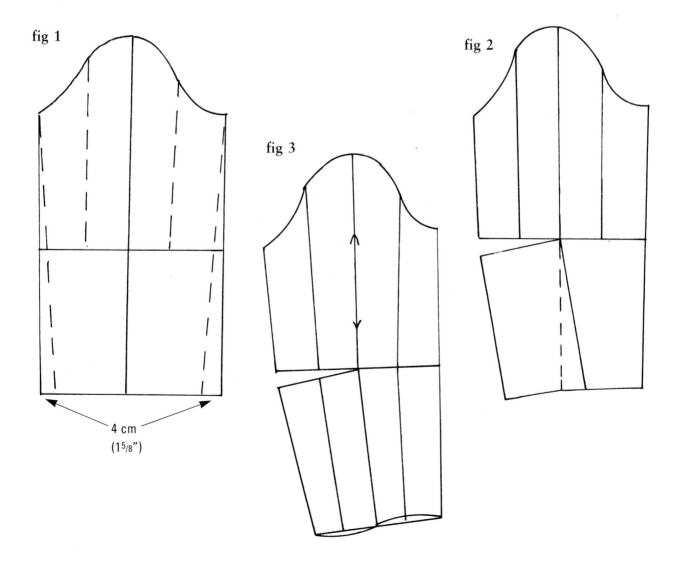

fig 1

fig 2

fig 3

4 cm
(1⅝")

Tightly Fitted Sleeve

This is a style seen only in bridalwear as it is too fitted for current fashions. It has been included because most dressmakers are asked at some time to undertake a bridal gown.

1 Take the original sleeve block and narrow the back and front arm lines as for the semi-fitted sleeve (p81).

2 Slash across the elbow line from the back seam to the front arm line, **fig 1**.

3 Fold out equally on the vertical lines up to the elbow line to reduce the width at the wrist to that desired, **fig 1**. This gives the dart shaping.

4 On the front seam at the elbow level, mark in 2 cm (³/4") and curve back to the armhole and wrist, **fig 2**.

5 Measure the total width of the dart shaping and divide the amount equally above and below the elbow, **fig 3**.

6 Divide into four at the wrist and draw back to meet front, back and top arm lines at the elbow, **fig 3**.

7 To add a bridal point, extend the top arm line by 5-6 cm (2-2³/8") at the wrist and draw back (see dotted line), **fig 3**.

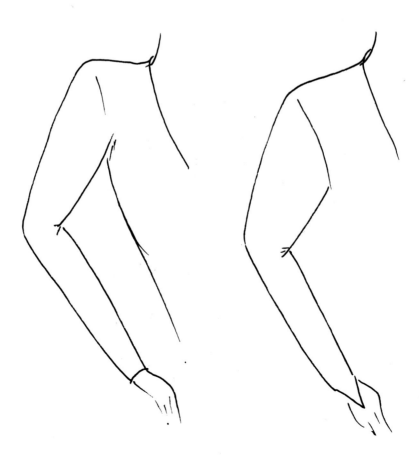

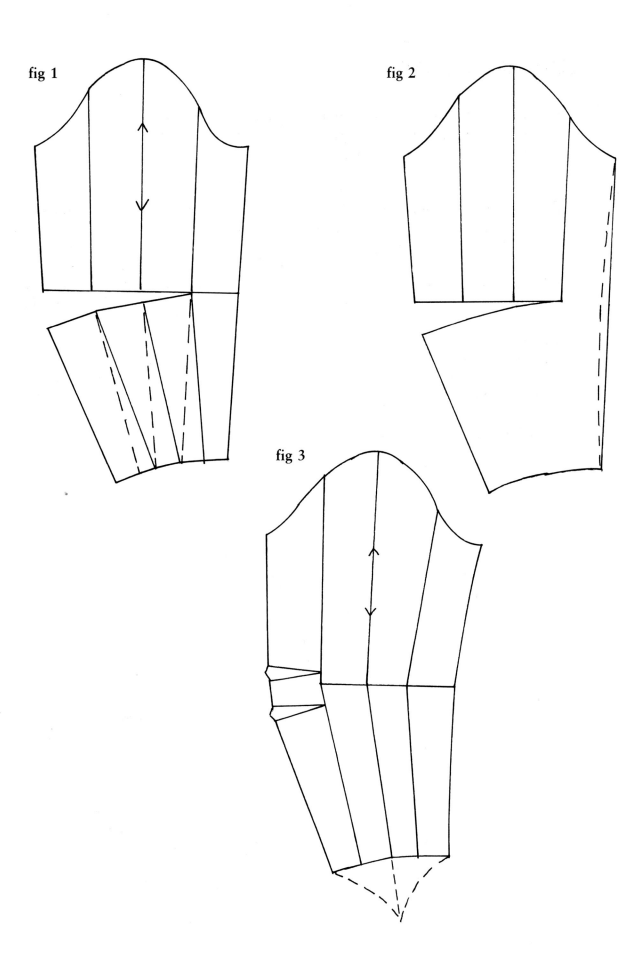

fig 1

fig 2

fig 3

Bishop Sleeve with Deep Cuff

The cuff may be as deep as required to complement the style of the rest of the garment.

1 Follow the instructions for the tight-fitted sleeve (pp82-3), up to opening up the elbow dart.

2 Mark in the style line for the cuff, **fig 1**, put in balance marks and cut away, **fig 2**.

3 Open the back arm line and add a buttonstand.

3 Square down the sleeve from the underarm and shape up and down at the hem, **fig 3.**

4 Using the shoulder point as a pivot, swing the sleeve out in both directions by approximately 8 cm (3^1/$_8$"), **fig 4.** Redraw.

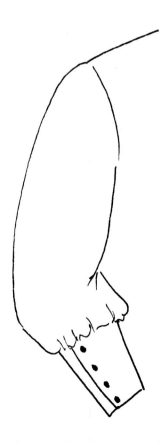
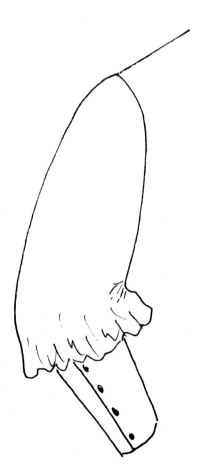

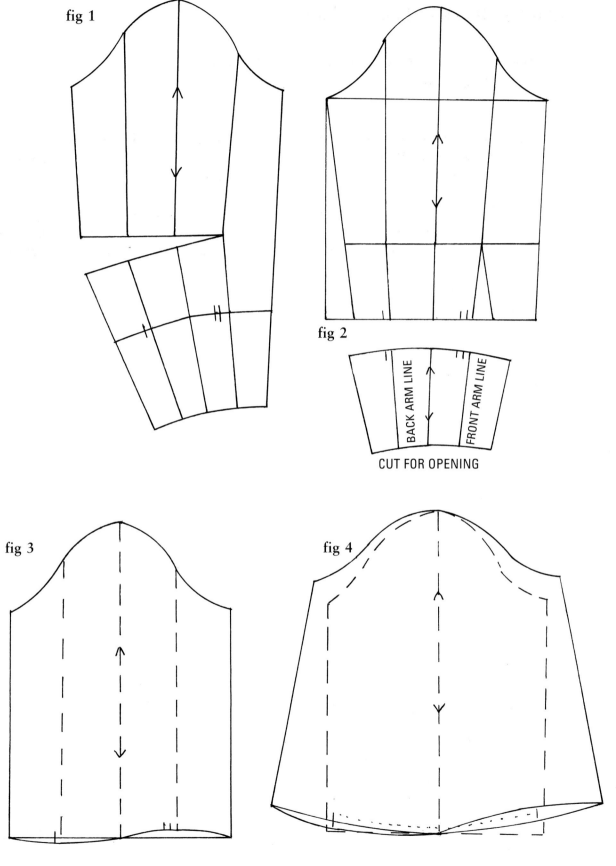

fig 1

fig 2

BACK ARM LINE

FRONT ARM LINE

CUT FOR OPENING

fig 3

fig 4

GATHER ALONG DOTTED LINE

Leg O'Mutton Sleeve

This style is most often seen in bridal or evening wear.

1 Start with a tightly-fitted long sleeve (pp82-3).

2 Slash right across the elbow line, **fig 1.**

3 Slash down the upper section of the sleeve along the vertical lines and spread for fullness, **fig 2.**

4 If a tighter wrist fit is wanted, fold out on the centre line and re-mark the vertical lines, equally spaced, **fig 2.**

5 Place the upper sleeve against the lower section. Do not overlap the sections or the sleeve will be shortened, **fig 2.** Redraw.

6 For a high, puffed sleeve head, redraw around the upper line. If a less raised head is required, use the lower line, dotted lines **fig 3.**

7 To give a more dramatic fit, curve in at the front elbow line and out slightly at the back, **fig 3.** Check the front and back seam are of the same length.

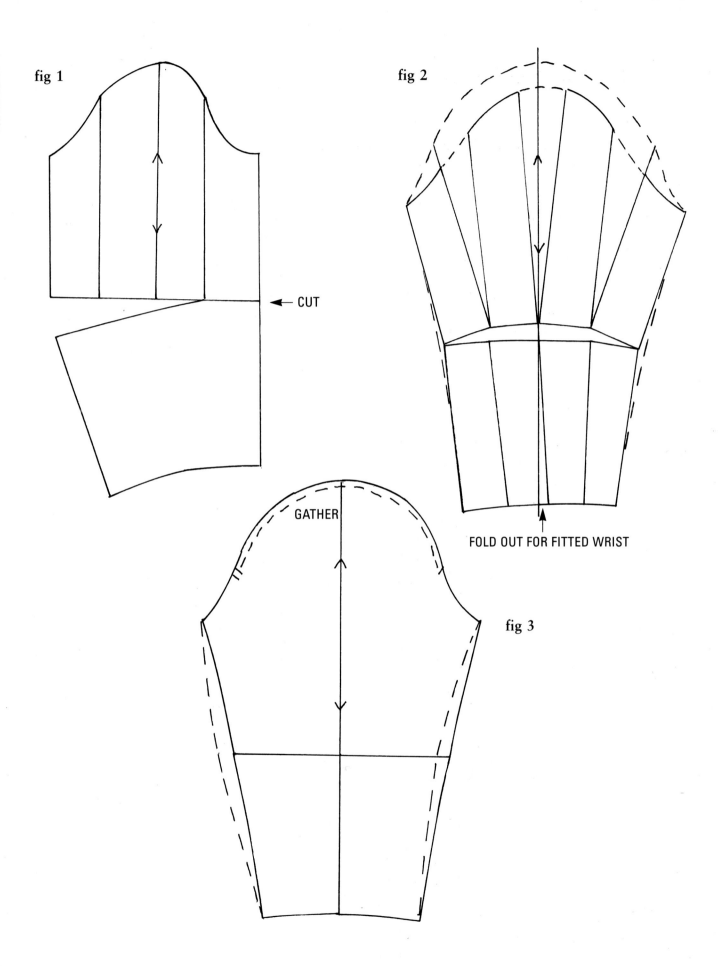

fig 1

← CUT

fig 2

FOLD OUT FOR FITTED WRIST

GATHER

fig 3

Raised Crown

This is a simple straight sleeve with a cuff, but the crown is raised. Variations on this design are popular for both daywear and outerwear.

In lightweight fabrics it may be necessary to support the raised head with some pleated net or similar.

1 Take the depth wanted for the cuff off the sleeve at the hem.

2 Outline the sleeve block, mark in the top arm line and draw two slightly diagonal lines from the beginning of the sleeve head curve, **fig 1**.

3 Slash down the top arm from the shoulder and out along the diagonal lines. Lift for fullness at the top, **fig 2**.

4 Redraw, marking the raised area for pleats or gathers, **fig 3**.

5 Cut a cuff the depth needed by the girth of the wrist plus 5 cm (2") ease, plus buttonstand.

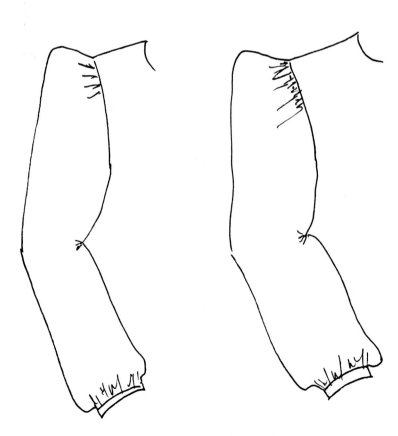

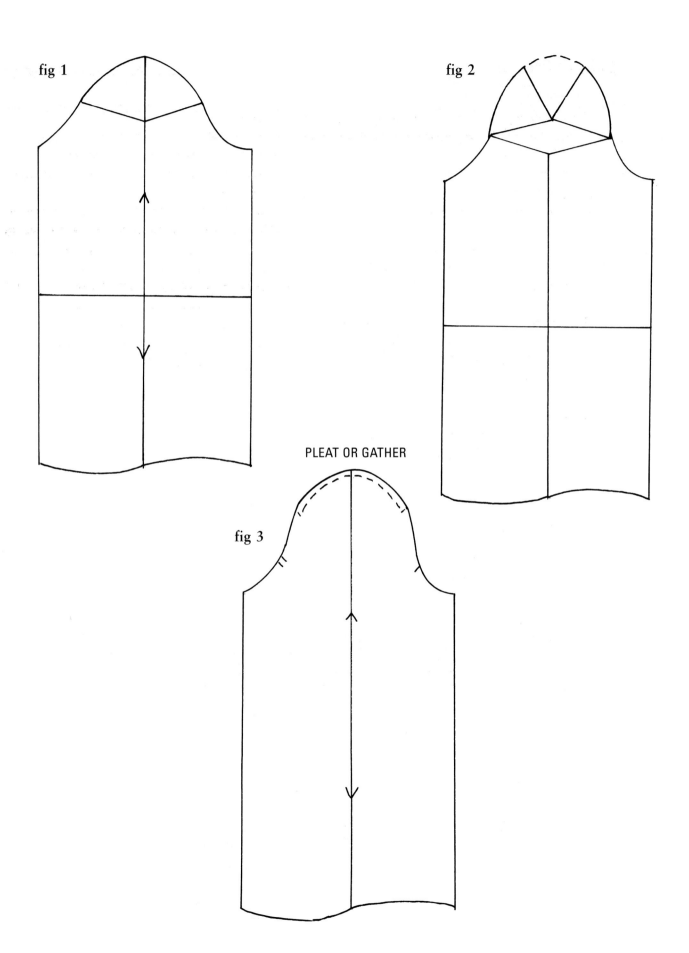

fig 1

fig 2

PLEAT OR GATHER

fig 3

Two-Piece Sleeve

The two-piece sleeve is normally used in outerwear.

1 Outline the straight sleeve and narrow it at the wrist by 2.5 cm (1") each side. Rule off to nothing at the armhole, **fig 1**.

2 Correct the position of the front and back arm lines, dotted lines **fig 1**.

3 Fold in on the new front and back lines to the centre and mark in lines 2.5 cm (1") from the folds towards the seam line, **fig 2**. Put in balance marks on both sections. Cut away on the dotted lines.

4 Cut across the elbow line from the back arm to the front, but do not cut through, **fig 3**. Spread the underarm section by 3 cm (1⅛") and upper arm section by 3.75 cm (1½"). Redraw.

5 On the upper sleeve, add 1 cm (³/₈") at each side of the under arm and curve off to nothing below the elbow. Correct the head, **fig 3**.

6 The garment armhole must be enlarged either at the shoulder or the underarm to accommodate the sleeve.

7 When making up, ease the fullness in the upper section at the elbow onto the under arm.

8 Straight grain is through centre of each pattern piece, **fig 4**.

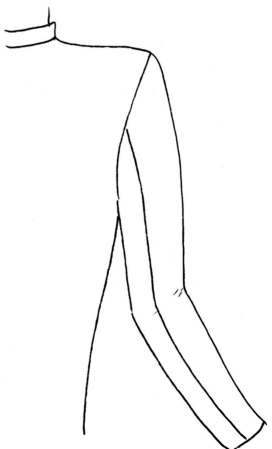

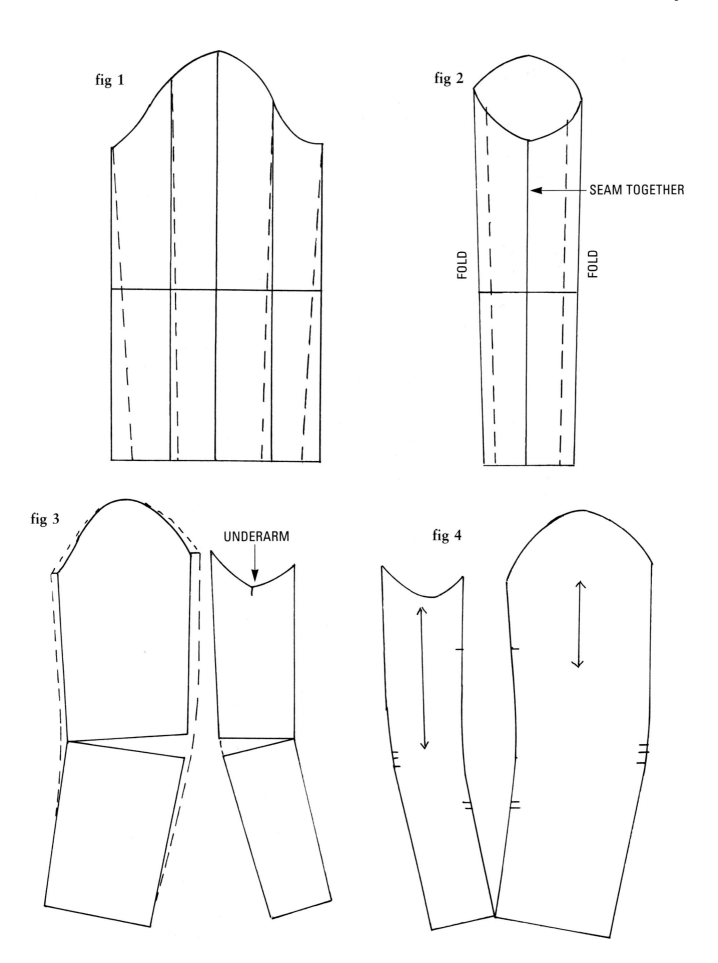

fig 1

fig 2

SEAM TOGETHER

FOLD

FOLD

fig 3

UNDERARM

fig 4

Plain Short Sleeve

1 Outline the block to an appropriate length and narrow at the back and front of the hem by approximately 1.5 cm (⅝") for a slimmer fit, **fig 1**. Check the seams are the same length.

2 Level off at hem. Draw a line 5 cm from the paper edge and fold under. Redraw the corrected sleeve pattern and unfold the paper for facing, **fig 2**.

3 For a sleeve with a cuff, cut away the facing pattern and double it in depth for the cuff pattern, **fig 3**.

4 Bag out over the sleeve hem and turn back for cuff.

Puffed Sleeve Gathered at Hem and Head

1 Outline the sleeve to the length required and mark into equal sections from head to hem, though not at the underarm, **fig 3**.

2 Mark a horizontal line across the sleeve and on a new piece of pattern paper. Slash through the lines and spread, matching the horizontal markers, **fig 4**.

3 Redraw, ensuring the balance marks are correct. For a gentle puff at the head, use the lower slash points. For a more raised head, take the higher slash points, see (see dotted lines), **fig 4**.

4 Final pattern, **fig 5**.

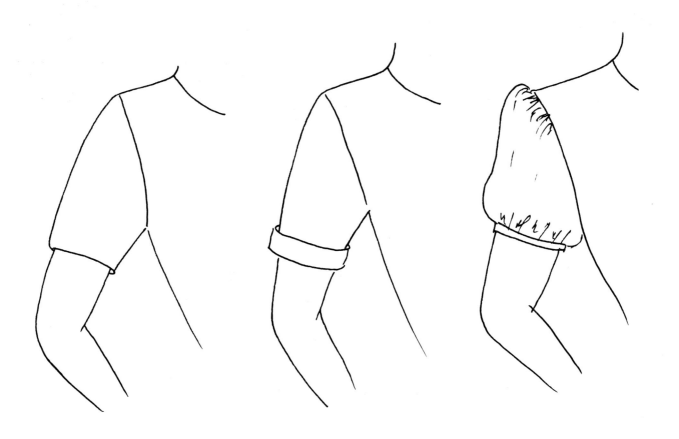

fig 1

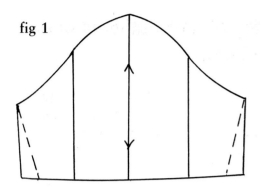

fig 2

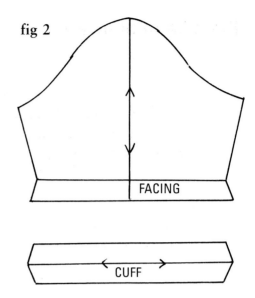

FACING

CUFF

fig 3

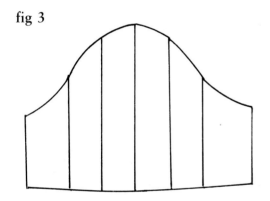

fig 4

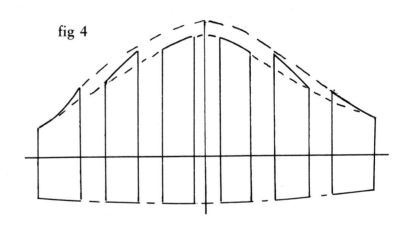

fig 5

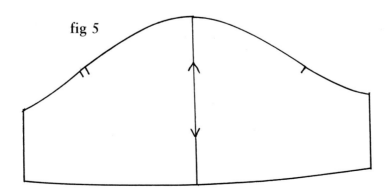

Bell Sleeve or Gathered Hem Sleeve

Either version of this sleeve fits smoothly at the head, with all its fullness at the hem.

1 Outline the sleeve and divide as for puffed sleeve (pp92-3), **fig 1**.

2 Cut up the lines from the hem to head, but do not cut through them, **fig 2**.

3 Spread at the hem for fullness, **fig 2**.

4 Correct the curve and redraw.

The gathering at the hem may be either into a band or onto elastic.

Sleeve Gathered at Head

1 Prepare the sleeve as for the bell sleeve, cutting down from the sleeve head but not through the hem, **fig 4**.

2 Spread for fullness and redraw, taking the upper or lower dotted line for a raised or flat gathering, **fig 4**.

3 Final pattern, **fig 5**.

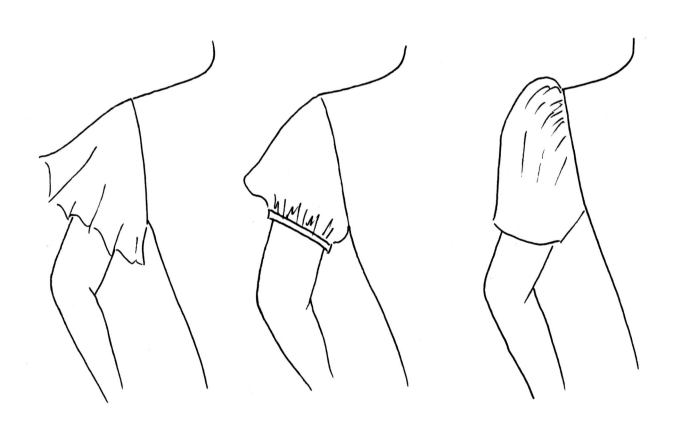

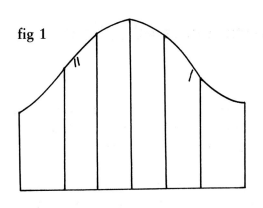

fig 1

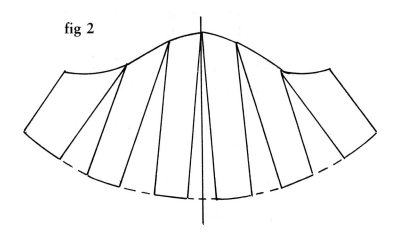

fig 2

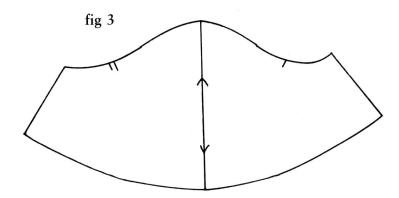

fig 3

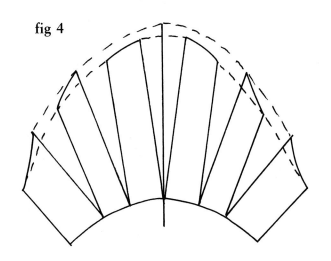

fig 4

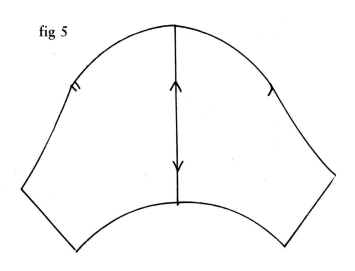

fig 5

Sports Sleeve

This has a loose fitting sleeve head, allowing for maximum arm movement.

1 Outline the front and back bodice and sleeve. Lower the armhole on the bodice by 1.5 cm (⅝"), **fig 1**.

2 Mark the three arm lines on the sleeve, **fig 2**.

3 Slash through on the front and back lines and spread both by 1.5 cm (⅝"), **fig 3**. Redraw.

4 Mark a curve from the shoulder point to the underarm and divide in two, **fig 4**.

5 Cut along these curves and the centre of the lines and lift to give a shallow sleeve head, **fig 5**.

6 Redraw, taking the underarm back to the original hem, **fig 5**.

7 Add facings. Final pattern, **fig 6**.

fig 1
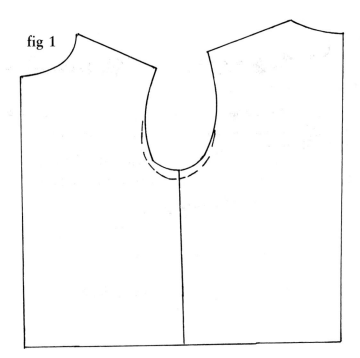

fig 2
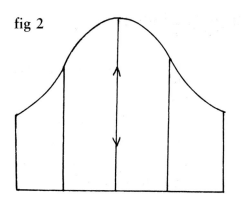

fig 3
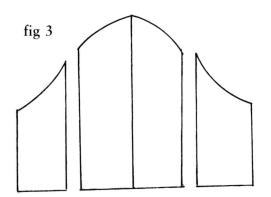

fig 4
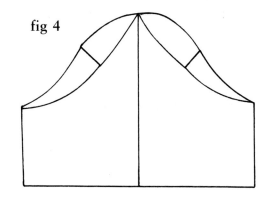

fig 5
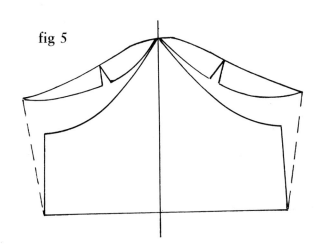

fig 6
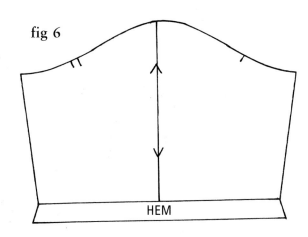

HEM

Saddle or Strap Shoulder Sleeve

This is a fairly casual style, usually seen with a loose-fitting garment. It is sometimes used as an alternative to the sports sleeve. However, if it is used for sportswear, extra width must be added.

1 Outline the garment front, back and sleeve blocks, **figs 1**, **2** and **3**.

2 On the back and front, draw lines parallel with the shoulder about 4 cm (1⅝") wide, **figs 1** and **2**. Add balance marks and cut away.

3 Mark the top arm line on the sleeve and extend this above the head by the length of the shoulder seam, **fig 3**. Attach the front and back shoulder sections either side of this line, **fig 4**.

4 Redraw with the straight grain on the top arm line, **fig 5**.

5 Soften the angle where the shoulder joins the garment, **fig 5**.

fig 1

fig 2

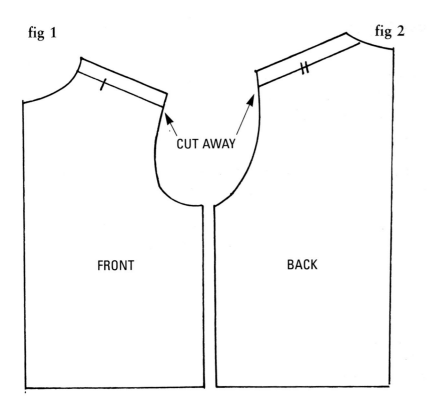

CUT AWAY

FRONT

BACK

fig 3

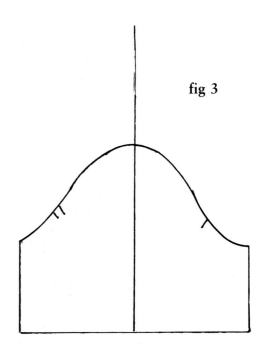

fig 4

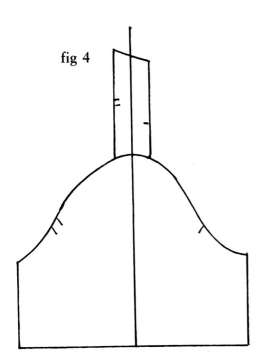

fig 5

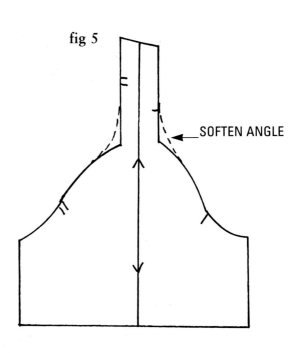

SOFTEN ANGLE

Kimono Sleeve

This is an easy-fit seamless block. The kimono sleeve was used extensively in the 1950s for daywear but is now more often seen in loose jackets, dressing-gowns or beach wraps.

This design is derived from either a dartless or an underbust darted block and sleeve, cut as one.

1 Outline the bodice block. Fold the sleeve down the top arm line and place against the shoulder point of the bodice, **fig 1**.

2 **Fig 1** shows three variations on this sleeve. The fit depends on the angle at which the sleeve joins the bodice.

3 For a snug fit it is vital that bodice and sleeve blocks do not overlap when drafting. A gusset is essential in more fitted versions to prevent tearing, **fig 2**.

4 The gusset is easier to apply if cut in two sections and added separately to front and back, **fig 3**.

5 Cut two triangles, of equal length on all sides (eg 5-6 cm [2-2³/₈"]) and insert.

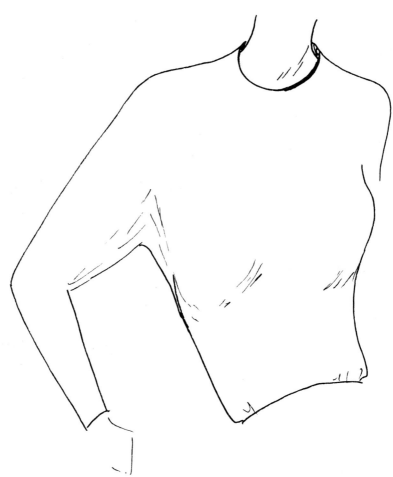

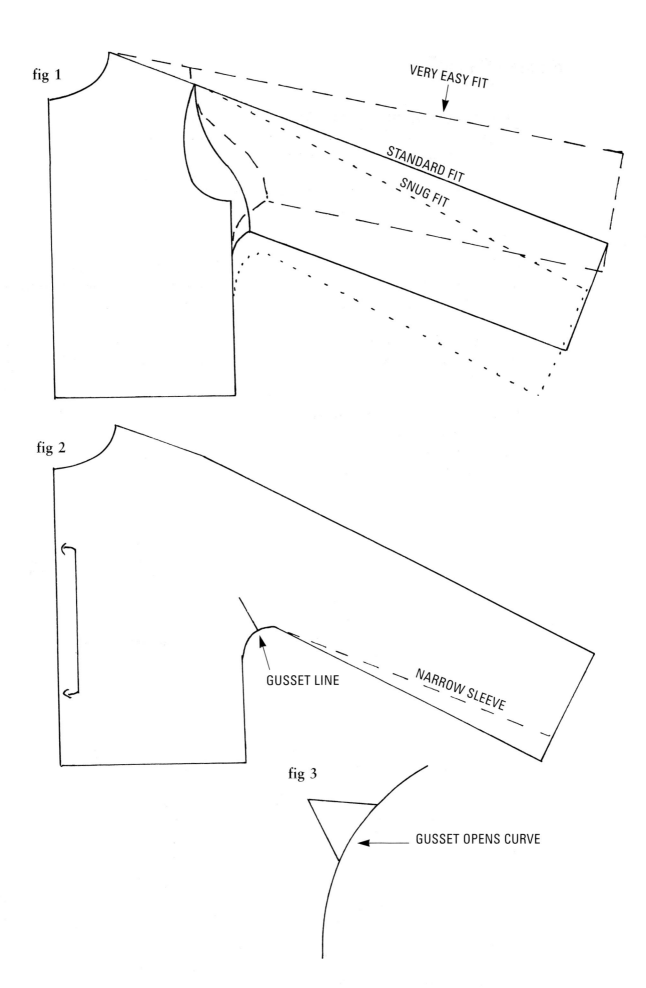

fig 1

VERY EASY FIT

STANDARD FIT

SNUG FIT

fig 2

GUSSET LINE

NARROW SLEEVE

fig 3

GUSSET OPENS CURVE

Deep Raglan Sleeve

This is an attractive and comfortable sleeve for easy daywear or for outerwear. It leaves plenty of room for extra layers underneath.

1 Using a snug kimono as a block, outline and draw in the raglan line from neck to underarm, **fig 1**. Add balance marks.

2 Cut away on the raglan line and add a built-in gusset to the front and back bodice and the sleeve, **fig 2**.

3 Sleeves may be cut in two pieces, with a seam on the top arm line, or joined and cut as one with the shoulder dart, **fig 3**.

4 If the style is cut from a straight shoulder kimono, there is no need for a shoulder dart (see dotted line), **fig 1**.

The raglan seam can be cut to any shape, but try the simple diagram shown here first.

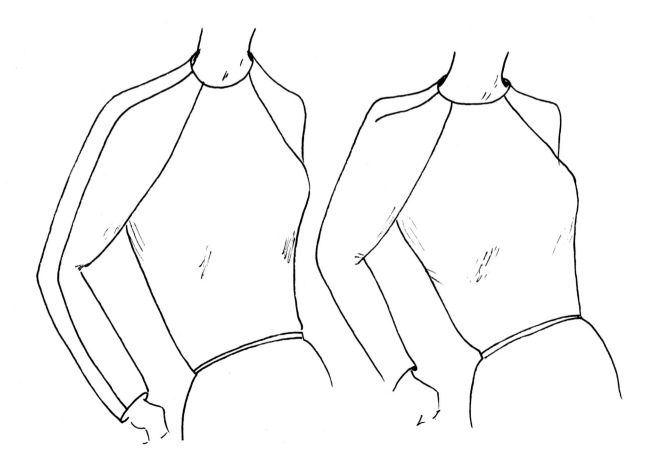

fig 1

SHOULDER POINT

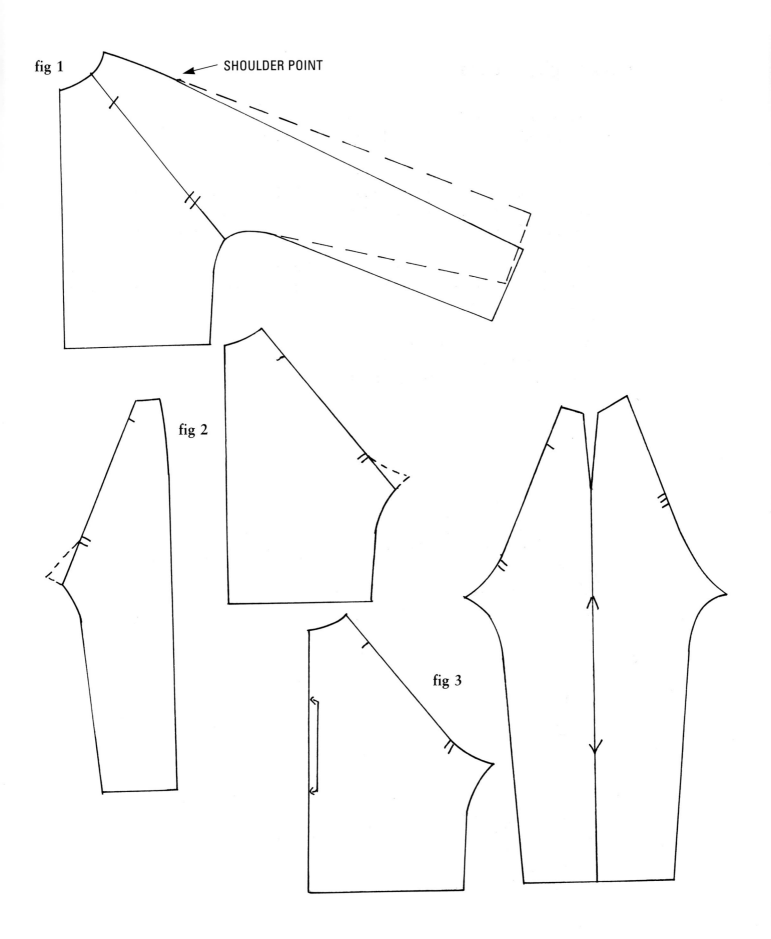

fig 2

fig 3

Cap Sleeve

Method 1

1 Raise the shoulder slightly from the neck point (by a maximum of 1 cm [3/8"]), **fig 1**, and extend for the cap by 8-10 cm (3 1/8-4").

2 Curve back into the underarm at the balance mark, **fig 1**.

3 This leaves the underarm sleeveless, preventing pull across the bust when the arm is pivoted.

4 Mark facings and trace off, **fig 2**.

Method 2

1 Raise the shoulder as above and draw up from underarm seam to join the shoulder, **fig 3**.

2 Add a gusset to prevent tearing across the bust. Cut a triangle, equal on all sides, about 6-8 cm (2 3/8-3 1/8"), **fig 3**.

3 Mark facings and trace off, **fig 4**.

4 Insert the gusset at the underarm seam, **fig 5**.

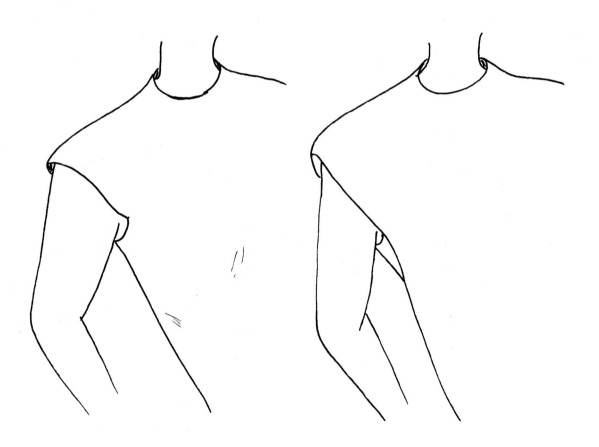

METHOD 1

fig 1

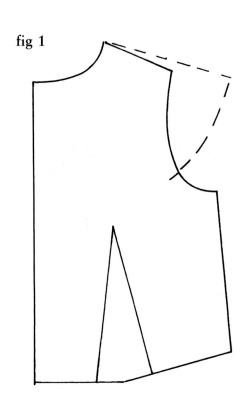

fig 2

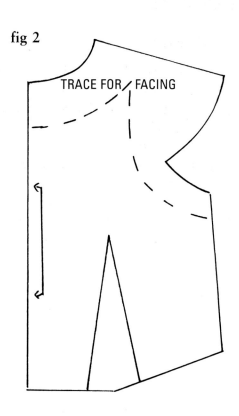

TRACE FOR FACING

METHOD 2

fig 3

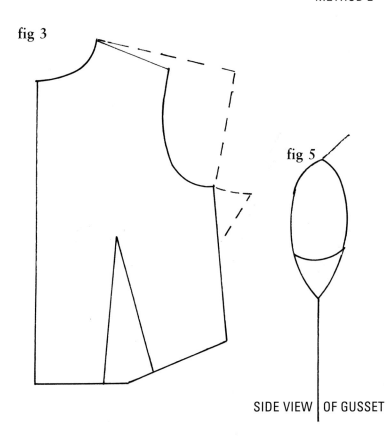

fig 5

SIDE VIEW OF GUSSET

fig 4

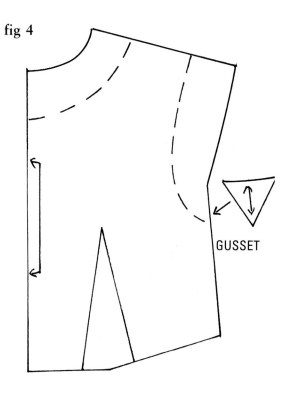

GUSSET

Hip Block

1 Outline the front and back bodice blocks and extend the centre front and back lines by the hip depth (see dotted line).

2 Square across by a quarter of the hip measurement, including ease.

3 Join waist to hip at the side seam (see dotted line), and soften the waist shaping from point A through the waist. Curve for hip.

4 Extend the underbust dart to 3 cm (1⅛") above the hip level and reduce the dart width by half to prevent creasing across the waist.

Jacket from Hip Block

Front and Back

1 Outline the hip blocks and lower the neckline by 3 mm (⅛") (see dotted line).

2 Extend the shoulder by 1 cm (⅜") or 1.25 (½") if using shoulder pads. This extension should be greater if using large shoulder pads.

3 Raise the shoulder at the armhole edge by 5 mm (¼"). Draw back to neck.

4 Lower the armhole by 1.25 cm (½"). Redraw the underarm curve.

5 Add 5 mm (¼") to the side seam.

6 For a loose fit add 5 mm (¼") at the centre front.

7 The dotted line shows the jacket outline.

Sleeve

1 Raise the sleeve head by 5 mm (¼"), more if using shoulder pads.

2 Slash and spread by 6 mm (¼")at the back and front arm lines.

3 Lower the armhole to correspond with the bodice.

Check that front and back bodices match at the side seam and that the sleeve head is about 2-4 cm (¾-1⅝") larger than the armhole.

Coat Block

Follow the instructions for converting a hip block for a jacket, doubling all the alteration measurement to achieve a basic outerwear block.

Pattern cutting for outerwear follows the same rules as for dress.

HIP BLOCK FROM BODICE

JACKET FROM HIP BLOCK

A

JACKET SLEEVE

SPREAD EQUALLY

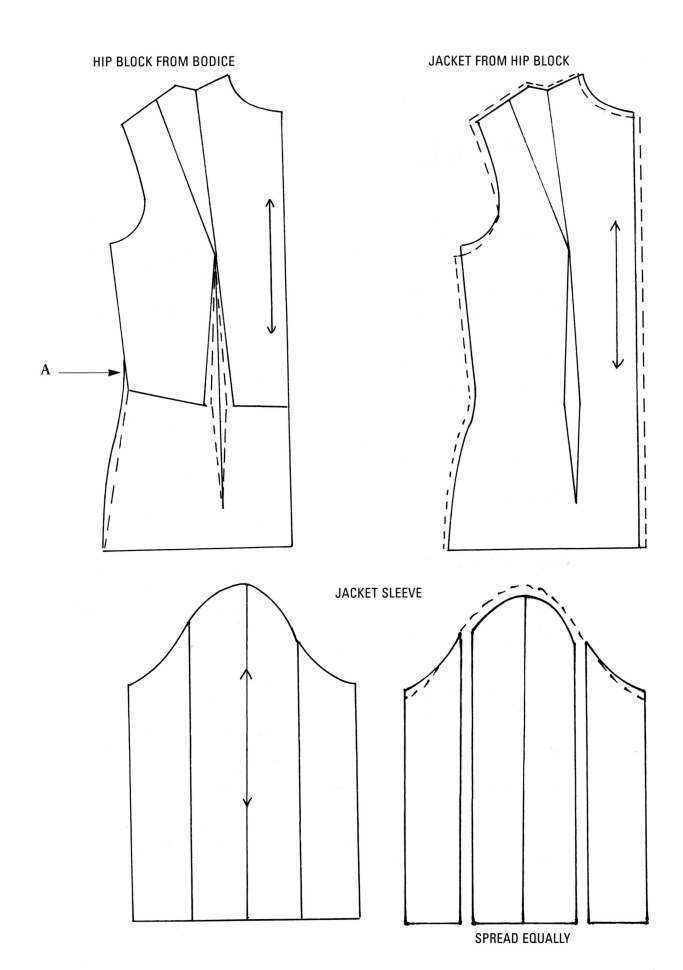

Tailored Collar

Used almost exclusively in jackets and coats, this collar looks more difficult than it is. Cut and constructed properly, with the undercollar slightly smaller than the top collar (so that the seam stays just under the edge), it will last for years. A good dressmaking book will give construction details.

1 Outline the block and add the buttonstand, **fig 1**.

2 Mark in the neckline, cut away and shorten the neck edge by opening the dart and folding it out on the line to the neck (as for V-Neck, pp 68-9), **fig 2**. Straighten the neck edge (dotted line).

3 Extend the neckline from the shoulder point by length of the back neck, **fig 3**. Square out for the centre back of the collar.

4 Draw in the collar shape or mark it on the garment, and trace, **fig 4**.

5 Slash down the neckline to the break point and lift for the collar stand by approximately three-quarters of the collar fall (see dotted line), **fig 5**.

6 Draw in a seam from back neck to break line, **fig 5**. Cut away, **fig 6**.

7 Cut the centre back collar to the straight grain fold. Mark the pattern piece 'cut 1'.

8 Cut the centre back under collar with the true bias to a centre seam. Its finished length is 5 mm (¹/₄") shorter than the top collar. Cut separate top and undercollar patterns to avoid confusion.

fig 1

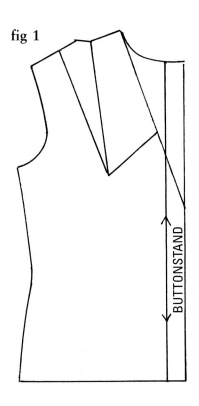

BUTTONSTAND

fig 2

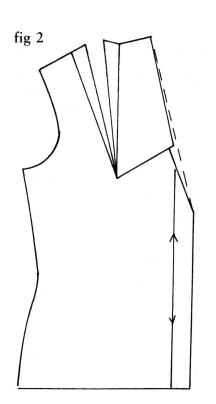

fig 3

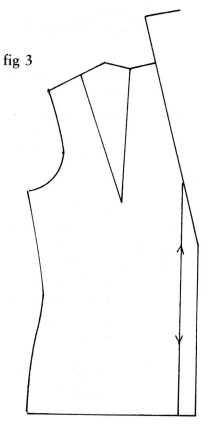

fig 4

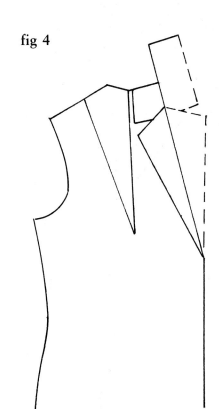

fig 5

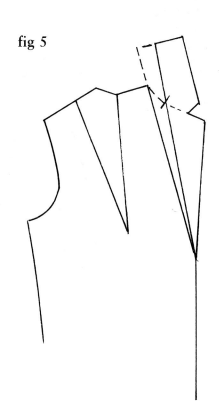

fig 6

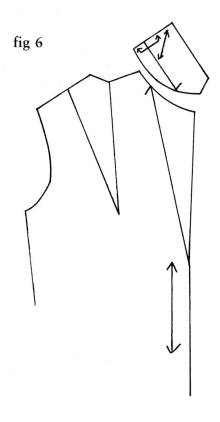

Trouser Block

Front

1 **A-B** Outside leg measurement, square across at both points.

2 **A-C** Hip depth, square across.

3 **C-D** Quarter hip including ease.

4 **A-E** Crotch depth, square across.

5 **E-F** Crotch line, equals C-D plus a quarter of this length. e.g. if quarter hip = 23 cm (9"); crotch line is 23 + 5.7 = 28.7 cm (9" + 2¹/₄ = 11¹/₄"). Curve back to hip.

6 **A-G** = C-D.

7 **G-H-I** Quarter of waist measurement, plus a 3 cm (1¹/₈") dart half way between G and H. Measure from G along the waist to H and up 1.25 cm (¹/₂") to I. Draw in waist curve.

8 **G-J** 1 cm (³/₈") in from waist, rule back to hip (dotted line). This provides a snug fit over the stomach.

9 **G-K** Square down from G to the floor.

10 **I-C** Hip curve.

11 For the outside leg curve, mark a vertical line 2 cm (³/₄") in from E-B and curve gently to knee.

12 For inside leg curve, mark a vertical line 2 cm (³/₄") out from D-K (see dotted line), and curve to knee.

13 When shaping at hem, the adjustments to inside and outside leg must be equal.

Back

1 Trace off front. Halfway between D and G, slash across horizontally and lift by 3-4 cm (1¹/₈-1⁵/₈"). Redraw. This prevents the waist dipping at the centre back when the wearer sits down.

2 At the crotch level extend the line at F by 2 cm (³/₄") and lower by 1 cm (³/₈") to L. Draw the inside leg back to the vertical line. Check the inside leg front and back are of equal length.

Once the trouser block is correct, the pattern can be adapted according to fashion, style and figure. Fullness can be added in the same way as in skirt cutting.

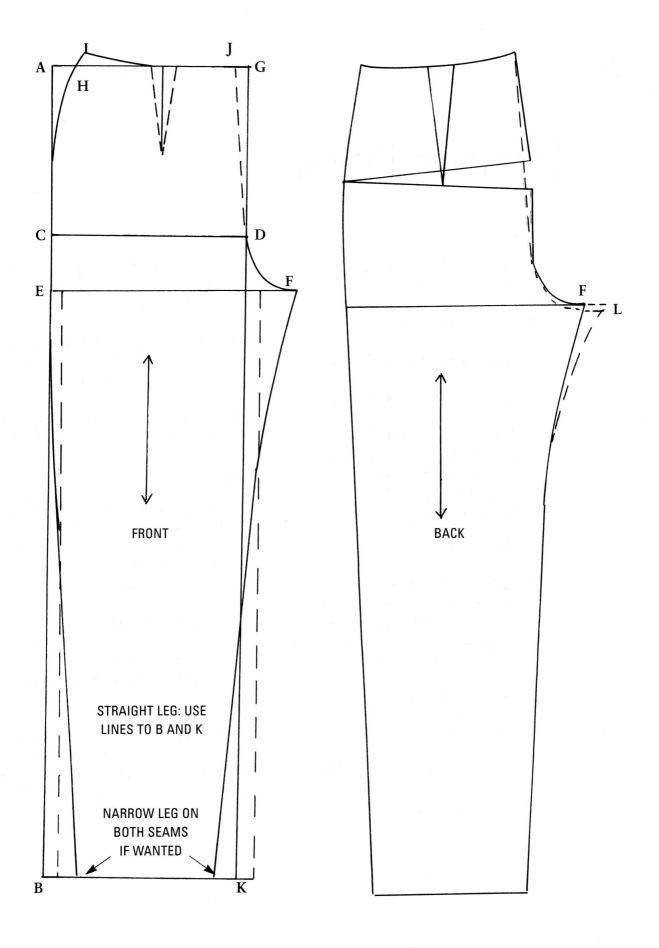

STRAIGHT LEG: USE
LINES TO B AND K

NARROW LEG ON
BOTH SEAMS
IF WANTED

FRONT

BACK

Pattern drafting and cutting, like any other skill, is easier and more successful with the correct tools. It is well worth investing in the following equipment:

Pattern paper, either plain or dot and cross. Plain paper in single sheets, available from MacCulloch & Wallis (address below), is often more convenient to handle. Dot and cross is usually only available in rolls which makes it heavy to lift.

Mounting card or stiff craft paper, for making the final blocks.

Fine line drawing pens. Once the pattern is correct, marking should be in ink so that it does not rub off.

A selection of pencils and a rubber.

Metre stick, marked with metric and imperial measurements.

Dressmakers or 'french' curve.

Grader set square with metric measurements shown both sides of centre.

'Notcher', for putting in balance marks.

Scissors that are easy to handle when cutting paper. They must give a clean cut. Do not use dressmaking scissors.

Craft knife, for cutting card.

Most of the above items are available by post from:

MacCulloch & Wallis Ltd
25 Dering Street
London W1R 0BH
Tel: 020 7629 0311

Morplan Ltd
PO Box 54
Temple Bank
Harlow
Essex CM20 2TS
Tel: 01279 435333

or 56 Great Tichfield Street
London W1P 8DX
0171636 1887
Tel: 020 7636 1887

R.D. Franks Ltd
Market Place
London W1N 8EJ
Tel: 020 7636 1244

R.D. Franks stock a very comprehensive range of books and magazines for fashion students.